Say YES Everyday!

Discovering your Superpower

Laura J. Brandao

©2021

Legal Disclaimer

ISBN 978-0-578-81411-7

Connect with Laura J. Brandao

https://www.linkedin.com/public-profile/in/laura-j-brandao-%E2%98%80%EF%B8%8F-80ab0444/

Visit us on the web: www.Sayyeseveryday.com

Email: laura@sayyeseveryday.com

Dedication

his book is dedicated to my parents, Robert and Louise Hallenbeck, who taught me to have no limits and the importance of family.

To my husband Tony for always supporting me and giving me the confidence to be unapologetically Laura.

And to my children Jonathan and Michael for giving me the greatest gift in life being their Mom and learning from you every single day.

Acknowledgements

My Say YES Everyday journey started the day that I was asked to moderate the top mortgage broker panel discussion at the first AIME (Association of Independent Mortgage Experts) event in March 2018. If that single event didn't occur, I never would have realized the power to get out of my comfort zone and Say YES Everyday. I am grateful that they saw something in me and didn't take No for an answer. They have also provided me with the opportunity to be part of the incredible Women's Mortgage Network. I have been in the mortgage industry for over twenty years, yet my world changed when I became part of WMN, and I now realize the power and importance of a tribe that supports you.

Once I started on my Say YES Everyday path, I met many people that lifted me up and showed me that I can make a positive change in the world that would create a ripple to others. My friend and colleague Christine Beckwith asked me to contribute to her book, *Win or Learn*, and provided me the opportunity to be a magazine columnist in her Women with Vision magazine. This gave me the confidence to start writing my own book.

Thank you to Dr. Andrea Pennington for being a contributor and sharing her personal story.

After I gained my writing confidence, it was time to figure out how to write a book, and that is when the universe brought me Larry Levine, who was initially a podcast guest, and is now a friend. He introduced me to my publisher, RTI Publishing, who gave me the gift of my first book, with a special shout out to Nancy Arnold for her advice and expertise with writing the book. You are a kind and wise woman, and I couldn't have done this without you.

I also want to recognize all of the amazing and inspirational Thrive Thursday guests (www.thrivethursday.org) who trusted me to share their unique superpowers. I have learned so much from each of you.

And finally, to my Mom who read every chapter, helped me edit, and has been there to mentor, guide and support me through my entire life journey. Although the book is a great accomplishment, the real treasure is the time that we spent working on it together. I will forever cherish this chapter in our lives, I love you!

Foreword

Do you yearn for a daily dose of inspiration? Has the weight of "unprecedented" circumstances worn you down? Do you struggle with accepting your own power to shine?

You are hereby challenged to Say YES Everyday!

Capturing a year committed to saying "Yes!" to any and all opportunities that came her way, author Laura Brandao has provided a north star for living one day at a time. A successful executive and breaker of glass ceilings, Laura transformed her goal of writing a book into a personal quest to change her life by accepting new people and new experiences each day, with open arms and without a second thought.

Laura is the president and only woman partner of American Financial Resources, a national mortgage company, and has earned countless business awards and industry accolades. To know Laura is to be both humbled and inspired. In her presence, it would be easy to sit silently in awe, but her enthusiasm is infectious, and her energy for empowering others to step up to challenges and define their own success is seemingly limitless.

Laura is passionate and collaborative, unaccepting of mediocrity or status quo. Laura is the kind of person you want to impress and will say "Yes!" to nearly anything she asks of you, simply for the opportunity to live up to the greatness she sees in you. Her energy creates a vortex you are honored to be pulled into – it matters not how you met, or where you are on your journey.

The best part is…Laura advocates that we *all* have the ability to discover our own personal superpower, and enrich each day by opening our life to step outside and accept new people and new adventures, without preconceptions or expectations.

Are you ready to Say YES Everyday?

Sheri Wachenheim

Table of Contents

Preface

L ife doesn't happen to us, it happens for us and it begins with the simple act of opening a door. I remember one of those life moments so clearly.

At 21 years old, I was the mother of a 2-year-old boy and working at a telemarketing call center in a starting position to supplement my family's income.

 I always knew that I was destined for a great life, regardless of the circumstances that I was experiencing. I knew that I had the power within me to create the life I wanted, and one of my dreams was for our family to own a home. I grew up renting, and after speaking with homeowners everyday while working on a mortgage telemarketing campaign, I decided that I would break the cycle and raise my family in a home of our own.

I knew I had to take action. So, one day I went to work early, so I could speak to the vice president of the company and ask to work more hours. Corporate protocol dictated that I should start by speaking to my supervisor. However, something inside me told me that the best approach was to go straight to the top.

I entered the supervisor's office and he was somewhat surprised and indignant that I would be so bold. He asked me what made me think I could just walk in and talk to him. I felt confident, so I simply told him the truth. I wanted to work more hours, so I could afford to buy a house.

My honesty and confidence seemed to change his attitude, and he asked me where I was thinking of buying a house. We made a connection in that moment and the relationship moved from cheeky employee and annoyed manager to his wanting to help and mentor me. That dynamic continued for many years as he continued to share his experience and insights with me.

I was promoted for showing initiative and continued to move along the path toward my goal.

I discovered that 'knowing what I want and asking for it' is one of my superpowers. I learned that when I act, while putting others first in the equation, I can successfully overcome fear and doubt and push forward to achieve any desired outcome.

Whether it is helping a client obtain a mortgage, or assisting my family and friends, when I am motivated to benefit those around me, nothing can hold me back.

It is important for entrepreneurs, especially, to identify their own superpower, and put it to work for them everyday. When you figure out your specific strength, you will know. Everything will feel right. You will find yourself "in the zone" where everything lines up, and it can feel almost magical. That is how you know you have found your own superpower.

I invite you to read on and let me help you find your superpower. I guarantee it is within you. Unlocking your superpower and being able to draw on it to achieve success in business and in life will motivate, inspire, and bring you the life you were destined to receive.

Together, we will explore how to quiet your negative inner monologue and help you to find the amazing and valuable person you are already. By uncovering the special gifts you were born with and learning to use them, we can get you started along your path to success and, hopefully, inspire you to take the knowledge you gain to help others around you to do the same.

Please come with me and we will find your gifts, open them, and unlock all the potential and happiness you have and deserve.

Laura J. Brandao

Chapter 1: My Life Was Ruined – or So I Thought

"Leadership is not about men in suits. It is a way of life for those who know who they are and are willing to be their best to create the life they want to live."
–Kathleen Schafer

Are you ready to Say YES Everyday and discover your superpower?

You Can Handle the Truth

You might think you are looking for happiness, but true happiness is temporary. No one can be happy all the time. The reality is, we are all seeking fulfillment. Discovering and using your superpower to positively affect and improve the lives of others provides you with a sense of purpose. Living into your purpose produces the feelings of fulfillment and happiness that we all desire.

When your superpower is shared with the world, there is a clarity that allows you to lose your ego. You are the conduit through which everything will flow. By focusing on the greater sense of good, and shifting perspective from "me" to "we," your legacy is formed. It's time for you to give yourself permission to discover and use your gifts to design the life you were destined to create.

I invite you to read my journey of how I found my superpower when I decided to Say YES Everyday!

Hear Me Roar

The first time I stood up to authority, I did it without a doubt and with the support of my family. I was responsible for a change in my high school curriculum, simply because I did not understand why swimming class was a mandatory physical education requirement. There were many high schools that did not have pools, and those students met all the graduation prerequisites. Why did I have to swim, if I was more comfortable doing another physical activity? I decided to ask for what I wanted, and I got it!

I remember how it all started. I came home from school, and I approached my mom and said, "I just don't understand why I have to take a swimming class." My mom is a strong leader and responded with, "If you don't think it's fair, do something about it."

At that moment, I got an idea. I decided to prepare a proposal and present it to the Board of Education to show them they will receive more engagement and participation if they allow students to select which physical education class they feel fits them best, instead of making swimming a mandatory requirement. My mother supported me and we presented our case during my first semester of my senior year. The Board of Education agreed. That one action was the impetus that changed the curriculum for all existing and future high school students in my town. That moment of success made me think law school could be in my future.

Saying "Yes!" to standing up for myself and others started a ripple effect that has continued to make waves. In that very board meeting, I realized the power of my voice and thought, "Well that worked out, how about I take it a step further?"

Since I was in my senior year of high school, I knew I had to start obtaining experience, if I was going to study law. I had already been accepted to attend Rutgers University, but now I needed to figure out how to get a job in a law firm.

Once again, I had an idea! I knew that the business students had access to a work study program, where they would go to class in the morning, and then work in the afternoon for credit and job experience. This knowledge led me to my next course of action. I went to the guidance office at my school to see if there were any work study jobs at a law firm.

The guidance counselor looked surprised when I asked him about finding a job via the work study program. He said, "You are already accepted into Rutgers University, why would you want to be part of the business track program?" He also told me that I was not eligible for a work study school program, because I wouldn't have enough credits to graduate.

Well, that did not make any sense to me, so I questioned, "How are the business students able to obtain enough credits?"

He told me they went to physical education class early in the morning to make sure they earned the mandatory credits. So, I said, "Perfect! I will take my PE class before school starts, and then I will meet all graduation prerequisites." He was surprised, and had no response for that, so we went ahead and scheduled an interview at a law office. I was hired on the spot.

Love Has Everything to Do With It

On that same day, December 1, 1988, I met my husband Tony. I knew from the moment we met we were going to be together forever. I listened to my intuition, and I asked him on a date. We are still together today and have two amazing sons.

I asked for what I wanted, the opportunity to interview for the legal job, even though they did not let college prep students utilize the work study program. I knew what I needed to do to get closer to my goal, and I was not going to allow an obstacle to push me off course. I stayed focused and if someone said "No," I would ask why, and then figure out how to turn their "No" into a "Yes!"

I followed my intuition and realized at an early age we only have individual moments of time. If you do not take action in the moment, you may miss your chance for love, success or true fulfillment. I knew Tony was the person on this Earth who could complete me. I was confident enough to ask for the date, and gained the love of my life, the father of my children, and a partner for life.

On my eighteenth birthday, Tony and I started planning for our engagement. He put my engagement ring on a twelve-month layaway, and on my nineteenth birthday, we had a beautiful evening together to celebrate. We had dinner at the Chart House, a lovely restaurant overlooking New York City, a carriage ride in Central Park, and a limousine ride. Tony got down on his knee and proposed to me while Kenny Rogers' "Crazy" played on the radio. It was perfect!

The Path Less Traveled

In December of that year, I found out I was pregnant. It was a shock that prompted some difficult conversations. Our parents, thankfully, were supportive and loving. After the phone call that confirmed my pregnancy, I had a moment where a voice inside told me I was supposed to have this baby and there would be greatness as a result.

I did not completely understand what that meant for my future, but the thought comforted me and made me feel this was supposed to happen, this way. Some people in our lives said things that hurt and dug in. The one I most remember was, "You just ruined your life." That stuck with me, and was a source of pain I carried with me. I had to work diligently to silence that negative voice.

I did struggle with being such a young mother. I felt judged and sometimes lied about my age to avoid questions and stares. When I look back now, I appreciate having my children so young. It worked well because I can now focus on my career and have my boys, too. I did not have to make that choice.

I came to understand that the message I received that night, as a frightened young woman expecting to start her family, was important. It told me my path was the right one for me, and I needed to follow it as it unfolded. I listened to that still, small voice, and it was correct.

I was a stay-at-home mom for a few years. Tony worked incredibly hard to provide for us, and give us a safe and comfortable home. I loved being with my first son everyday and celebrating every milestone and new achievement as he grew.

Back in the Saddle

I thrive on social interaction and being around others. So, I found a way to fit work back into my life by working nights. There were definitely times when Tony and I felt like we were two ships passing in the night, as he came home and I handed him two kids and ran off to work until midnight. But it worked for our family. You know when you are in the middle of a challenging time, it feels like it will never end. Looking back at that time in my life, I recognize that it was so valuable. That crazy, exhausting, tag-team parenting period gave me the ability to nurture and shape the lives of my children, while developing skills that I needed for my future career as an executive.

The only evening jobs available at that time were retail stores or telemarketing. The telemarketing job interested me because I could work nights when the kids were sleeping, and I could choose to take inbound calls or make outbound calls. I chose outbound. People thought I was crazy, but let me explain.

Inbound calls meant I would be sitting and waiting for the phone to ring. That did not appeal to me at all. I preferred to take action and to make something happen. I also realized that I am very competitive, so the bigger the challenge, the more I enjoyed the work. I followed my personal philosophy of setting my own work pace and environment, and not just going along with what others wanted from me. Even at a young age, I knew that the path less traveled would provide a greater reward in the future.

The Gift You Are Given

When you are a child, you believe you can do or be anything you can imagine. As you get older, the world and reality begins to intrude, and you lose faith in yourself and the path you might have chosen. By following the same routines day in and day out, you dull your ability to grow and learn.

We are all born with a special and unique gift. There is something you are meant to do, and you have the innate ability to accomplish that purpose. Discovering your gift, and learning to use it to better yourself and the lives of others, is all about saying "Yes!" to new things everyday and opening yourself to new experiences.

The true power comes when you apply your gift in everything you do, both personally and professionally, and combine it with others' unique gifts. We all need to release our gifts into the world and say "Yes!" to sharing them. We all have the power within us to live out our destiny, once we stop repeating the same routines and events over and over again. Remember you are a unique individual with an exclusive superpower configuration just waiting to emerge. It's not in the future, and the power is not with someone else waiting to give it to you. It's up to you to glow from within, and grow and be your true exceptional self. Everything you want or need is within you right now! The more you give, sharing your unique gift with the world, the more you will get.

Nice Girls Don't...

I have found, for women in particular, many people advise you to tone it down or keep quiet to be feminine. You are reminded that being driven, passionate, and opinionated may be construed as aggressive and shrill.

Young women being told these things may start to believe them. That is a shame, and can cause them to give up their dreams, because they are led to think they cannot get there by being themselves.

I had my aha moment when I realized Laura Brandao was put on this Earth for a reason, and I was no longer going to "Tone it down!" I will ask for what I want, and I will use my gift to get what I need to help others.

I have discovered that it is important to share my gift to help others find the confidence to find and use their superpowers.

Remember never dim your light for others. Use your voice and share your gifts with the world, and if someone is just not ready to receive your message, it's okay.

Ask and Ye Shall Receive

I have come to realize that once you discover your gift or superpower, asking for what you want becomes easier and it begins to feel natural. Others will begin to say "Yes!" to your requests, even when it doesn't make logical sense. Leaning into your personal superpower causes things in your life to align and fall into place. Denying your gifts and holding back will result in you missing out on events and relationships that you deserve, and are destined to be in your life. Hiding your superpower is a disservice to who you are and why you were born.

When you find the gift you were given, you can begin to trust it. The more you use your gift and share it with others, the easier it becomes to take control of your own path.

For example, you might not meet a certain person until it made the most sense in your life to do so. The meeting now has a clear purpose rather than being a random occurrence. Remember you can't see what you have, until you step outside your routine, so you may need to change your environment and surroundings to realize your gift. Go somewhere you haven't been, and answer the call for adventure, even if it's just a different drive to the office or a walk in the park. Changing your perspective, and quite literally, your view of the world, can unleash answers that you may be searching for at this time.

Confidence

I think people do not understand they have the power to create the life that they have always envisioned. Many people go through life simply reacting to what happens to them, instead of stepping forward to take the lead and carve out their own destiny. As we travel on the road of life, we begin to view our lives from the lens and perspective by which we are looking out. When your perspective shifts, a new horizon may come into focus, and your life will adjust to it. This is a blessing because it means that we can view our circumstances how we choose.

Personally, I go into every situation knowing that it will turn out in a positive and successful way. Now, don't get me wrong, it doesn't always happen; but in my mind, success is the end result. And when it's not, I'm ok. I don't change my thinking; I just go to my Plan B to work toward the result I'm looking for. I am also confident that if something doesn't turn out the way I expected, it may just not be the right time, and I stay open for it to occur in the future.

Life is full of unexpected occurrences. Having the confidence to proactively move toward your vision, and control how that movement progresses, is about being able to ask for what you want and plan your next step.

It all starts with visualizing what you want your life to look like. I find that this is a substantial struggle for some people. It goes back to your perspective. Some of us don't think we are worthy of having a life without drama, because we haven't seen that life before. But, guess what?

You can have what you can see in your mind, and what you say out loud to others, even if you come from a family or household that had a lot of drama. You can ask for what you need to help move you along your desired path, by first understanding that you have the power to do so, and you deserve the things for which you are asking. You get one life, and what you make of it is up to you. Why not reach for the stars? Remember you don't have to copy what the world has communicated what a best life is. You get to determine your own definition; and no one can define your "good" or "best" other than you.

Finding Your Tribe

My experience of being a young mother shaped my view on finding my tribe. When I was nineteen and interacting with much older mothers, I found it difficult to fit in. I did not have much in common with them, and I struggled with feeling they might judge me and find me 'lacking' somehow.

When I moved into management, I quickly understood I could not be friends with my staff. There had to be a level of separation to make the dynamic effective, and keep the work on track, so I did not socialize with my staff outside of work. Although I knew it could be a lonely existence, I knew it was the right thing at the time.

For many years, I didn't have a tribe. I had my husband, sons, and family, and I was busy with work and raising my boys. There was little time to feel alone, but it was lonely, all the same.

I realized I needed friends in my life, too. I needed other women I could talk to, and laugh and cry with when things were crazy or wonderful. I needed to find my friend tribe to fill this gap in my life.

I now understand that I couldn't let others into my life until I was showing my authentic self. Once I began to Say YES Everyday, I removed my defensive shell that was created by years of competing to be the hardest-working person in the company, taking on every task because I thought that was the way I could fulfill all of my career goals. As I started using my superpower of lifting up others, I tore down my walls and started letting others in, which resulted in supportive, flourishing friendships that I will continue to treasure.

The greatest gift I've received from my new tribe is the happiness I get from watching them grow and succeed. I have won awards and felt pride in my accomplishments, but that feeling cannot compare to the satisfaction of watching a friend spread her wings and soar, whether it's for the first or fifth time.

Find Your Joy

You need to choose the life you want, because remember, only you have the power to make changes that will impact every facet of your time here, and make it the best it can be, everyday.

Being open to new ideas, situations, and challenges can provide options for you to make choices that bring you joy and fulfillment. The key is to take control and form the vision of what you want your life to be, and then take the steps to get where you want to go. You must ask for what you want. Be brave, be bold and be confident.

Be-YOU-tiful!

What I would like my readers to take from this journey with me is to find the courage to discover your own superpower, learn how to use it, and make everyday a new, wonderful, and joyful experience. My hope is that by sharing what I have learned, I can empower and support others in their travels along the road of life.

Laura J. Brandao

Chapter 2: You Are Not What They Told You

"Man is a creature who lives not upon bread alone, but principally by catchwords; and the little rift between the sexes is astonishingly widened by simply teaching one set of catchwords to the girls and another to the boys."

— Robert Louis Stevenson, *Virginibus Puerisque*

A Good Start

My first job in the mortgage industry was with a mortgage broker that originated loans by cold calling potential clients. Once the outbound telemarketing team created interest, they would connect them to loan officers to have their mortgage applications completed. The loan officers would determine which loan program was the best fit, and work with the client to obtain the best interest rate.

I was hired to create and build the outbound telemarketing team. I was responsible for staffing the department, and training new hires on how to create interest and form relationships with our prospects.

On my first day at the broker shop, I met Melissa. She explained to me that she just hired a new receptionist for the firm, and she still had a large list of hopeful candidates who might be potential hires for the telemarketing department. That list was a gift. I managed to hire fifteen people from that list and did not have to place one "help wanted" advertisement.

Now, let's take a closer look at this example. There's more than one way to look at this. Some might see it as just a fluke or a chance happening; or, we can look at it as a gift that was put there for me to use, so my new venture would be successful. This is where I want you to open your mind and realize that these little gifts are appearing all around us in our lives, but a lot of times, we are so consumed with the day-to-day that we miss them.

Unfortunately, if you don't act, and receive the gift intended for you when it presents itself, it will pass and not return. Open your eyes and your ears, because these gifts are there for you, so you can use your superpower to have a positive effect on others. See, I not only put myself on a great career path, I brought 15 people who had applied for a receptionist job on a new path of mortgage sales. That's the power we have, when we use our gifts.

My new inside sales department ended up being so successful at getting hot leads from their cold calls, the loan processing department wasn't able to keep up with the number of families in process. My team overperformed, and I could see the other team was struggling. I saw a problem that needed a solution.

Problem Solved

I decided the fastest and easiest way to solve the problem was to train my team to process loan paperwork. This took some pressure off the loan officers, and kept the company making a profit by not having to turn business away. I asked the operations manager to train me to process loan files. Then, I trained my team to do the same. This is also how I learned the skills that would enable me to become a COO in the future.

My plan was successful and here came another one of those "gift," By this time, Tony & I had bought a house; so, we had a mortgage, two kids, etc., and Tony was still working two jobs. He would get up at 3 am to go deliver newspapers six days a week, then come home and shower and work from 8-4, then come home and take care of the kids, while I went off to work nights.

Although it was challenging, we knew we had to stay the course if we were going to provide our family with the life that we envisioned. But remember, I was using my superpower of building others up and empowering them to feel confident. So as a result, things were falling into place. One evening, I was working with my new inside sales team, and the owner of the broker shop came in with an older gentleman, John. Keep in mind, I was only 26 years old at the time.

He was bragging to John how I was able to hire and train fifteen new-to-the-mortgage-industry team members, and they were generating so many leads that they couldn't keep up with the production. The older gentleman asked if he could speak with me, and for the next 90 minutes, I answered his questions and shared my philosophy on how to manage teams with him. At 9 pm that night, John decided to join the company as a partner, he promoted me to Chief Operating Officer, and he gave me a $20,000 per year raise on the spot.

Now, the strangest part of this story is that I drove home that night so excited and proud of myself, and when I opened the door to my house, Tony was waiting for me. I could tell something wasn't right, so I asked, "Is something wrong?"

He said, "Yeah, I received a call from the supervisor at the newspaper. They are closing our local office and we were all laid off, effective Friday."

So, here I am coming in the door with the news of a promotion and a raise at the exact same moment when my husband lost his job, making almost the exact same amount of income. That is the power of using our gifts!

The Big Chair

For eighteen months, I was the Chief Operations Officer and worked hard to keep the teams efficient and productive. Then, the economy turned, and the mortgage business entered a difficult downturn. My company was not immune, and our new client numbers declined.

I got a call to speak to the CEO. I clearly remember walking in and noting he was seated behind a huge desk in a large chair. The guest chair in front of the desk was tiny in comparison. He asked if I knew why he had such a large desk in his office, and went on to explain it denoted his power position.

He told me the size of the furniture showed he was the big man, and the other person in his office was of lesser importance. This rankled me. I sat on the edge of that small, wooden chair with my back straight and my head up as high as I could manage. I was not going to be cowed by this demeaning strategy.

The CEO went on to explain he was taking away my $20,000 raise, because he had never personally agreed to it and the market had taken a turn. He said the other owner had decided on my raise, but he did not feel I was worth that much salary to the company.

Take This Job and...

I listened to his statement, and I did not hesitate in my response. I stated that if he proceeded to reduce my salary from the amount I had been promised, I would leave the company immediately. I explained I would make sure my team had everything they needed, and I would depart at the end of the day.

I refused to be told by anyone I was lacking in worth. I did not call my husband before quitting. I did not need to. I knew Tony would support me, and he did. He asked what I would like to do next. I told him I was going to contact another gentleman who had previously offered me a job that I turned down.

I made that contact and was hired straight away at a salary higher than the one I was making at the mortgage company, including the raise. I want every person who reads this to understand that no one can tell you that you are not worthy of anything. You are worth so much more than you take credit for. Never let another person tell you that you are not worthy or valuable…because you are!

Sugar and Spice and Everything Nice

I have interviewed many women throughout my career. One theme that runs consistently through every dialogue is the conditioning girls receive when they are growing up. Many women seem to have been told from childhood that it is important to look their best, take care of others, and be nice and nurturing.

I was not brought up that way. I was always told my only limits would come from me, and I could do what anyone else could do. While I understand what other women have been told, and what they have told me, I find it an unnatural position.

From a very early age, I was inventive and creative. While many girls in the neighborhood talked about style and hair, I found my place with a group of younger boys who would play school, and take direction from me everyday on my back porch. I innovated at school, and suggested new music and plays to my fourth-grade teacher, and the whole class participated in my Christmas and Easter plays. I never wanted to sit on the sidelines and just wait for something to happen.

Little girls are told to sit quietly and listen to others, while little boys are free to run about energetically, and be boisterous and loud. That messaging influences us later in life, when men are more likely to step forward and speak up for themselves, and women may hold back or stay quiet, instead of taking the spotlight.

I have observed women are more prone to evaluate a problem or situation strategically, while men may step in quickly and aggressively, more willing to accept unknown risk. I do not necessarily see this as a negative. Taking a measured approach can be prudent and wise. However, if it is simply a product of conditioning and not always appropriate, being over-cautious can result in lost opportunities.

To-may-to, To-mah-to

When a woman states her position loudly and strongly, she may be called aggressive. When a man does the same, he will be called assertive or powerful. Men talk about their accomplishments and are lauded for being confident. A woman who speaks of her success may be labeled as braggadocious.

I almost feel that, as a woman, you are supposed to speak about your kids and your family life. If you talk about business, it may be construed as being neglectful of your children and home. Men are not held to the same standard. They are expected to be the "king of the castle" and occupy themselves with more important matters than groceries and PTA meetings.

There is a clear double standard that becomes glaringly apparent when women feel they need to choose between a career and family. No matter which way she turns, a woman will be criticized for her choice. If she chooses family, she has ignored her potential; if she chooses work, she is somehow less of a woman.

I would like every woman to realize that you do not need to choose. You one hundred percent have the opportunity to have it all! As long as you come to the realization that although you have a superpower, you are not a super woman, so surround yourself with a strong supportive network. Your partner, your family, your friends and your community are vital assets, essential to you being fulfilled. Please remember asking for help is not a weakness, it's a strength. You got this!

Also, for our men, it's ok to embrace your softer side. Years ago, you had to show your power and bring your ego front and center, but those days are gone. Being supportive and creating a collaborative diverse environment for your teams will allow everyone to flourish.

Here She Is... Miss America

I interviewed a young woman that was going to be a speaker at a women's event I was arranging. She was 27 at the time, had her MBA from Stanford University, and was a co-founder of a tech company in Silicon Valley. I was surprised when she asked if she should mention that she had been a contestant in the Miss America pageant.

I asked why she thought that would be an inappropriate item to mention in her remarks. She was concerned because some women in the audience might take offense. She worried they might see her as less worthy for having entered a beauty pageant to get scholarship money for her education.

I explained that what I felt was wrong was not how she got her scholarship funds, but the fact that she felt judged by others for how she accomplished that goal. She was helping others with her choice, by not saddling her family with student loans and debt.

This young lady also told me some friends were freezing their eggs to make sure they were able to have a family, should they choose to pursue a career first and wait to have children. It made me realize young women are being asked to choose one or the other. Whereas, for men, the freedom to have both in their lives is not a choice, but a given.

What it Takes

It takes a confident man to partner with a strong woman. He needs to be comfortable with himself and feel he can give her what she needs. He also has to be able to look after himself and fulfill his potential, while supporting how she works on herself. If he lacks confidence in himself, it can be an opening for resentment and disappointment for both of them.

A man who constantly tries to prove himself to others

and puts up a front of false bravado cannot be an equal and supportive partner to a woman who knows her worth and is able to ask for what she wants. That woman needs someone at her back, just as she will have his, when needed.

It Starts in the Cradle

Ultimately, how boys and girls are raised, and taught about their worth and potential, has a huge impact on their success and accomplishments as adults. For the most part, boys are raised to assertively and confidently speak out and ask for what they want, without the fear of being labeled as aggressive or pushy.

When a girl is told in childhood that it is more ladylike to stay quiet, demure, and motherly, despite her desire to attain her goals, whatever they might be, there is a barrier erected that boys simply do not have to get past to succeed.

My upbringing taught me I was worthy and capable of chasing my dreams. I have a husband who supports that wholeheartedly, and I am passionate about teaching the next generation of girls to ask for what they want. If you do not ask, you will never know the confidence and pride that comes with stepping up and forward for yourself.

I want girls to know that feeling. I want to stop the cycle

here, with this generation, and raise the next generation of girls to be strong, confident, and successful - not despite their gender, but because of it. I ultimately feel that women have an advantage as leaders, because they not only have the business expertise, they also have strong relational skills and emotional intelligence. But we must support our girls and our women team members to give them the confidence to use their voice, and take their seat at the table.

Chapter 3: What Is Your Entrepreneurial Superpower?

"I know I am a valuable asset to the world. Today I hold the highest vision who I am and why I am here."
- Andrea Pennington, M.D.

In Her Words – Dr. Andrea Pennington

I am an American citizen currently living in the south of France. My mother immigrated from Southern Guyana to the U.S. in the 1960s. She divorced my father, and I grew up with her and my brother and sister. Our home was post-Victorian and children were expected to stay quiet and still most of the time.

I grew up feeling as though I had no right to speak, and yet I was a performing artist. I played the piano and people would tell my mother how pretty I was, but no one ever asked me what I was thinking or feeling. They never wanted to know what I had to say.

When I discovered theater, I found a place for my voice to be heard and to express my true self. My mother was supportive and was always present at my recitals and performances. Being in front of an audience led me to discover my superpower.

My superpower is my huge heart of compassion. I realized when you are forced to sit quietly and just observe those around you, you learn to read their body language and energy and get to know them that way. I was able to discern when someone was being honest, or if they were holding back or being dishonest.

Over time, my ability to see into others' hearts became more proficient and I could also see when someone was suffering. I could sense it in their movements and the energy they put forth.

I do not know whether I was born an empath or became one because of my upbringing. Probably because of a little of both, I developed a strong desire to help people end their suffering and break free of what was making them feel unwell.

I did not see a lot of my father as I grew up, as he had moved to another state. We did spend time together on holidays and we talked frequently on the telephone. He grew up in a poor family, so making a good living to support yourself was high on his list of priorities. When he asked how I was doing in school, he actually wanted to know about my grades.

My father gave me a keen sense of needing to achieve. With that need came what I now recognize as imposter syndrome. I knew my dad would still love me, even if I did not get straight As. However, I had developed a need to be perfect and to live up to everyone else's ideals. I never felt good enough or that I had done enough.

I discovered if you work against your true nature, you may have success but it will never feel fulfilling. The pressure I put on myself made me suffer a lot of anxiety. I had achieved success as a writer and on television, but I still felt depressed and unable to cope.

I took a vacation in the south of France and decided to introduce myself as Draya the artist. No one knew me there, and with that anonymity I could express myself through music instead of medicine. I met a person on the beach who invited me to sing at a club that evening. I went and had a wonderful experience. I sang to the audience and had a moment of utter euphoria.

While I was singing to that sea of people, I felt like I was my authentic self. I was accepted, loved, and felt a state of bliss. I woke up in my hotel room the next morning still happy and content, until I remembered that two days later, I was expected to return to my other life of work and media, with many people depending on me.

I started to cry and felt as depressed and lost as I had ever felt in my life. I fell on the bed with my eyes closed and my body seemed to melt into the mattress. Suddenly a bright, intense light enveloped me. I was confused as to what it was, but I could feel myself searching for it. I was drawn to the light and began to feel at peace.

I saw a vision of my future life. I was walking on a beach holding the hand of a child and I was a professional singer. At that moment, I seemed to slip back into myself and my depression and anxiety had gone. I understood I had a choice of how my life would proceed. It had been my own choice all along. With that realization came peace and calm.

I started to research my experience and found it was not as uncommon as I would have expected. Many people had similar episodes of spiritual awakening from different sources and triggers.

After discovering my authentic self and being able to understand my choices and how I could be the architect of my own life, I spent fifteen years researching mystical experiences, consciousness, brainwave entrainment, and other types of enlightening incidents to help others reconnect to themselves and achieve and retain a state of self love.

I have learned to use my abilities to help others and provide them with the tools they need to be themselves and find happiness and fulfillment, as they were meant to experience it in their own lives.

Winning...

Meeting Dr. Pennington was another great example of why I Say YES Everyday! I heard her message, it resonated with me and I took action to connect with her. I have meet so many wonderful people this past 18 months. One of them is Shawn Harper, a former NFL player who taught me that everyone is born a winner. The odds of a unique individual being created and born are astronomical. If you understand how special and specific you are, you will understand you are born winning from the start.

I believe there is a reason why you are created for this world. You have a purpose for being here in the time and place you arrive. If you were the same as everyone else, and had no individual gifts or thoughts, humanity could not survive. There would be no innovation, discovery, or imagination. The world would be colorless and stagnant.

The greatest thing you can do is say "Yes!" to your life purpose. When you share your gift or superpower with others and blend them together, the combination renders everyone more powerful as a community.

The creation of positive energy when you share with others helps to stimulate innovation, momentum, and a ripple of more positivity across global society. This movement begins with you realizing there is a reason you were born and added to the human race.

Even when negative things happen, you need to take them not as finite conclusions, but as lessons for moving forward again. Bad situations can be the gateway to better times, if you are able to see them for what they are and work to put yourself back on track.

Seek and You Shall Find

There are steps you can take to discover your superpower and start sharing it with the world. First, I would like to clarify what I mean by "superpower." Some people will confuse a superpower with a talent, like painting, music or sport. Those are wonderful attributes to have, but they are not the superpowers to which I am referring.

Your superpower is innate. It is something born into you that is given to you for a reason. It is deeper inside you than a talent that you can hone through practice and repetition.

Your superpower can be suppressed by repetitive action. It only shines in its true form when you share it with others and use it to make the world a better place for everyone. Your superpower is unique to you and special, because it can only be uncovered with introspection and experience.

Toe the Line

When you are young, at school you are taught to hold back and obey the rules. You are encouraged not to disrupt the status quo, and to follow an established pattern of behavior like everyone else. The problem is that this discourages you from exploring yourself as an individual.

To find and use your superpower to its full potential, you must first open your mind and heart. You need to trust your intuition and not allow routine and rote to shadow the truth. When you are open to learning about yourself and your reason for being, and able to explore those reasons freely, your purpose will become crystal clear.

Time Will Tell

I have found through research that many people do not find their superpower until later in their lives. There are things that need to be taken care of, which can get in the way of the journey of self-discovery. The basic needs of life need to be met before there is extra time. You need food and shelter, and work to feel secure and meet the needs of your children.

The next thing you know, you are in your mid-40s. Then you will begin to have the time to go deeper into yourself, and shift your attention to the more esoteric parts that have been neglected while you were distracted by the more mundane, but necessary, activities in life.

I asked my hairdresser, Tracy, if she had discovered her superpower. She felt it was how she made her clients feel special. She would make them look beautiful and feel good about themselves. She also recognized it was not just her talent with the scissors, but her positive and encouraging manner that helped her clients to be happier when they left her chair than when they arrived.

You might not tap into your superpower early in your life, but that does not diminish its impact when you find it and begin to share it with the world. It would be better if people discovered their light earlier, rather than later in life. However, if it brings happiness and fulfillment when one's superpower appears, that is ultimately what is most important.

The Magic of Use

When you have identified your superpower, it is vital to use it as much and as often as possible. It is like a muscle; the more exercise it gets, the more it grows and becomes powerful.

Your superpower comes from deep within you, and it will come naturally from your heart, without thought or artifice. You will want to use it more often, and in an ever-widening circle, as you meet new people and open yourself to new situations.

Others will be attracted to your superpower like moths to a flame. Their gift may resonate closely to yours, drawing you together. Your superpowers may mix to become an even greater force for good.

There was a cartoon in the 1970s called the "Wonder Twins." It was about siblings who had their own superpowers, but those powers only activated when they were together. The combination of the two provided the catalyst for the powers to come alive.

Many people enjoy superhero stories and films. You come to realize that each hero has their own power, but they also have a weakness. That weakness may be exploited by malicious forces. However, when the heroes come together to fight as a team, each strength can compensate for another's weakness and make the whole group stronger and invincible.

There is a feeling of "wholeness" that comes with sharing your superpower with others, and having them share theirs with you. The power that emanates from you when you share your gifts with an honest and open heart is virtually unstoppable, and makes life much sweeter for everyone.

The splendor of sharing your superpower can be compared to a symphony orchestra. When the instruments combine with their different timbres, tones, and pitches, the result is music that can soothe and stir the soul of those who listen. If one instrument is out of tune or missing, the melody is diminished without the supporting harmony.

Dr. Pennington

This chapter began with my colleague, Dr. Andrea Pennington, describing her journey of discovery to find her superpower and purpose in life.

Dr. Pennington came to my attention when I saw her TED Talk and heard her story. She fascinated and inspired me. I admired her ability to connect with patients on a visceral level, and help them by alleviating more than just their physical pain. She opened her mind to more than conventional medical practices, and was able to improve her patients' lives in many ways.

Dr. Pennington leaned into her superpower and uses it to make a profound difference in the world. She eschewed the traditional path for one that is intuitive and heart-centred.

She makes a difference in the world and her success has gained my respect and admiration.

I want you to learn from Dr. Pennington's willingness to recognize, accept, and use her superpower. I want you to know you are special, and have a reason and purpose you may have not yet discovered. Open yourself to honestly and willingly understanding how much of a miracle you are and are empowered to become.

Laura J. Brandao

Chapter 4: The Confidence Factor

"Confidence isn't optimism or pessimism, and it's not a character attribute.
It's the expectation of a positive outcome."
– Rosabeth Moss Kanter

"We're Not Worthy..."

A lack of confidence will make you shy away from opportunities that present themselves in many areas of your life. If your thoughts turn to your unworthiness to accept the gifts you are offered, then you need to adjust that mindset or success will elude you. This is why it's so important for you to use your superpowers; because the more you share them with the world, you will build confidence because you are no longer competing with others or comparing yourself. Why? Because there is only one of you in this world, and our lack of confidence comes when we feel less than someone else. But, it is essential to recognized that you don't need to be the best in what someone else does, because you have your own unique gifts.

When your confidence is low, you might not be able to put yourself on the path of the amazing things life can offer.

You choose to stay on the sidelines because you do not feel capable of accomplishing certain tasks, or participating in activities will diminish your chance to experience life in all its amazing textures and layers.

When you have a limiting belief, you see everything through a "need of validation" filter. You wait for someone else to tell you that you are good enough and that you deserve to have the opportunity to proceed.

One unintended consequence of needing that kind of validation is that you may choose to spend your time with others lacking vision or drive. Doing so might make you feel better about yourself in the short run, but will ultimately lead to limiting yourself from having more, and becoming the best version of yourself. Remember you never want to be the smartest or most successful person in the room, you always want to keep striving to be more.

You Are Not the Father...

The Jerry Springer Show is a good example of how you can limit yourself by holding up a mirror to others, instead of challenging yourself. It seems many people admit to watching shows like Springer's because they think their lives cannot be as bad as the poor souls that end up on the stage, humiliating themselves and airing their dirty laundry for the world.

The problem with that type of thinking is that it promotes the mistaken impression you are elevating yourself by looking down on others. That castle is built on sand, and will eventually have its foundation washed away, leaving you without a firm footing of confidence in yourself.

An absence of confidence can lead to second guessing decisions. This, in turn, can be a frustrating and ultimately limiting experience. When you are confident in yourself and your abilities, you can make a decision and follow your decision through, even if it ends up being wrong. Confidence provides the strength to learn from mistakes, and not let them become an overwhelming obstacle to moving forward.

Confidence Is....

I define confidence as a feeling of certainty. It is feeling you can trust your gifts and abilities, and you are sure of who you are as a person.

Having confidence means you can believe in what you are good at, and, at the same time, not let inexperience or a known weakness limit you from trying new things or saying "Yes!" to new opportunities. It is a positive state of mind that allows you to attempt new things without fearing catastrophic failure.

If you know you are proficient at something like singing, public speaking or mathematics, you can share that gift with others and know it will be of value and may help improve their lives or situations.

Confidence allows you to share your gifts and trust they will allow you to provide a positive contribution and be of benefit to those around you.

The Myth of Perfection

Confidence can also be the recognition and acceptance that you will not be good at everything you try (and ,that is OK, too). Confident people are willing to step out of their comfort zone and try something unfamiliar, sure in the knowledge that, even if they fail, they will learn something. They recognize lessons learned are valuable, as well. They can ask for help and support from others, when needed.

Why Do You Lack Confidence?

I have discovered the following factors can cause a lack of confidence: biology or genetics, culture, and childhood experience or trauma. Confidence can be elusive for some people as they grow and mature into adulthood. It is certain, however, you can overcome insecurity and become sure of yourself in new and important ways.

What Did You Expect?

One common reason for a lack of confidence is setting unrealistic expectations for yourself. When you approach a situation or opportunity with the mindset of an absolute need to be perfect and to succeed immediately, you are setting yourself up for failure and disappointment.

In the same vein, unrealistic expectations can also prevent you from saying "Yes!" to new experiences, by assuming a failed outcome is predetermined and any attempts are futile. People who lack confidence may not push themselves to try new things, because they give up after one unsuccessful attempt. They cannot bring themselves to chance having that same outcome, even though it is not guaranteed a failure would result from trying again.

When we say "Yes!" everyday, the minute you do something new, or look at things through a clear and positive lens, you have already won and taken an important step toward feeling more confident in yourself. If you can accomplish that with a reasonable expectation, you will have gained even more in the attempt.

Judge Not...

You are your worst critic. I doubt I could find anyone who would tell me they have not been disappointed in

49

themselves at one point in their life, and judged themselves unworthy.

Another aspect of this self-castigation is your perception of being judged by others. The truth is that, while you may spend a lot of time and energy worrying about how others see you and may judge what you do, those people are more likely worrying about their own issues.

In other words, they are not concerned with what you are doing and are more concerned about what they are experiencing in their own life. Comparing yourself to others is unproductive and can damage your confidence to the point you are stalled from getting what you want out of life.

Turn Off the Screen

Social media is a prime example that promulgates this damaging mindset. When you peruse Facebook or Instagram and start comparing your life and activities to those of others, you can begin to feel inadequate, or like you are failing to have a "perfect" life. You see smiling faces in family photos, beautiful crafts and meals being presented, and lovely family vacations.

You might read about unexpected promotions, new cars, and weddings, and feel you have somehow missed the boat on these exciting parts of life, if you do not have the financial resources to get them, or the large circle of friends filling your social calendar.

The reality is those pictures are the highlight reels from someone else's life. They are a snapshot that encapsulates a moment in time, but not the struggles to get to that point.

I have found women tend to judge themselves more harshly than men. Women can be so prone to feel automatically negative about themselves that the mirror of social media can be destructive, and cause considerable unhappiness in those who take it to heart as a reflection of their perceived failures.

Find Your Own Joy

If something brings you joy, continue doing it! Focusing on positives and the smallest successes builds confidence. If you want to strengthen your muscles, you must exercise them. Confidence is like a muscle. To make it strong and have it carry you where you want to go, you need to keep building up your confidence everyday.

Finding something that gives you joy can build that confidence muscle, by letting you do something you love and want to accomplish. Hopefully, that will lead you to something new, and enable you to approach it with a more positive outlook.

The Bamboo Tree

Chinese bamboo seeds can take up to five years to sprout. They lie dormant in the soil, but with watering, fertilization, and care, they will break through the earth and then reach rapidly for the sky. Bamboo grows at a breakneck pace once it gets started, and can provide an abundant, continual harvest for many cycles. It is a wonderful example of how patience and persistence can pay off.

Confidence can be like bamboo. It may be quiet beneath the surface and hidden from view. But when it is nurtured and encouraged to reach for the light, it can explode and grow strong and vibrant. The trick is to be patient with yourself. Find the right soil and fertilizer to care for yourself. Be willing to open yourself to the sun, and let yourself flourish as you are meant to, with trust in yourself and your abilities.

Float Like a Butterfly....

Something that brings me joy is our annual family tradition of planting milkweed on our property. We do this to encourage monarch butterflies to visit. They rely on milkweed for food, and to shelter their chrysalis while they are undergoing their magical transformation from caterpillar to butterfly.

We plant the seeds around Mother's Day, and then look after them through the summer. We water, weed, and nurture the plants, so they will be ready for the monarch caterpillars to arrive, feed, and weave their little bundles within the fresh, green stalks.

This year, I worked from home and waited all summer for the time to come. I watered and watched and was disappointed when nothing came. I needed to be patient. They were late this year, but I had lost confidence in them. It seemed when I waited patiently, they finally came.

Confidence needs work and faith. It requires you to be patient and hold onto your trust in yourself, even if success takes longer than you expect. Like the bamboo seed or the monarch caterpillar, good things will come if you believe in yourself and set your expectations realistically. It might not be on a set schedule, but the joy will come, if you believe in it.

Bringing it Back

You cannot expect something to change, unless you are willing to change it yourself. You can regain lost confidence by deliberately saying "Yes!" to new things everyday, and allowing yourself the leeway to make mistakes and still say "Yes!" again. Every time you say "Yes!" to something new, you will get a boost of confidence, and it will grow at a steady rate.

Once you begin to say "Yes!" regularly, it becomes easier to do. Turning off the filter of fear will remove the limitations you have placed on yourself. Every win, no matter how big or small, will add to your confidence and allow you to step up to the next challenge with a greater expectation of success, and less trepidation, should the attempt be unfulfilling.

Have a mindset of abundance. You can have the things you want in life, if you let yourself try and reach for them. Turning away from a challenge with a mindset of fear and unworthiness will limit you, and lead to nothing but regret and unhappiness. Remember you have everything you need within yourself to create your best life. Regardless of any labels or titles you have worn previously.

Have Fun

Everyday is a gift. You only get each day once; when it is over, it is never going to come back. So why not live each day with joy and let fear go? Why not have a day of being the best person you can be, and put your mark on it?

Confidence can be the ability to wake up every morning and think of all the possibilities for that day. I encourage you to not take life so seriously, and look at each new day as an adventure that you can control. We all have our regular duties, work, chores, and attending to your family's needs. But you also get to decide how you are going to do each task, and I implore you to choose adventure and joy! There should be more to your day than going through the motions. Love each day because you are filled with infinite potential that must be shared with the world.

Finding the Solution

Every entrepreneur will face obstacles in their path to success, and will need to solve problems. Confidence will allow you to trust that, for every problem you encounter, there will be a solution. It may not come immediately, or in the form you expect. But it will present itself, if you believe it is out there.

Having a clear head and focusing on the positive is essential for solving issues and moving forward toward your goals. I have found when I concentrate on the answer, rather than the problem, the answer is far more likely to appear.

The bottom line is letting yourself feel good about the things you do, even when they do not always result in success, is key to building your confidence and allowing yourself to throw off limitations and fear.

Once those veils are removed, you will find your ability to enjoy life and enrich your work, relationships, and accomplishments is boundless, and can benefit you, as well as your family and friends. By sharing your confidence, you encourage others to find their confidence, and the positive cycle will continue. Remember we are not on this Earth to beg or wish for our greatest life. We are here to come into a great sense of gratitude and humility for the gifts that we have, and to celebrate what has been given to us, so it can be activated and funneled through us, so we can create limitless greatness in the world. Stop asking and hoping that something will happen and come to the realization that you already have what you need. You were actually born with it.

Chapter 5: You Can Be More

"The great secret of getting what you want from life is to know what you want and believe you can have it."
—Norman Vincent Peale

I Have an Idea

On my twenty-ninth birthday, I made the decision that by the time I turned thirty, I would have my own company. I had no idea of what kind of company I would have, but I had a goal and was determined to see it come to fruition. At the time, I was the director of sales for a wire and cable company, but I wanted more. I wanted something of my own.

One Sunday morning, I went outside to get the newspaper as was my normal routine. On this day, however, I was suddenly aware of a tiny voice inside telling me it was critical I look at the want ads. I was not looking for a job, but I have learned to listen and trust this voice. I took the paper inside and spread it out on the table to have a look.

My eye was drawn to an ad for a director of sales in a night-time telemarketing department. I was surprised to see the person in charge of hiring for the position was someone I had interviewed with a few years ago. I had not taken that job, but I guessed this must be the sign my still, small voice was pointing me toward. Remember when I said women have great relational skills? This is an example, make connections and be memorable, because you never know when you may need to connect puzzle pieces in your life.

I called him the next morning and arranged to meet at his office. I told him I was not interested in the job being offered, but I would appreciate having a chat with him. He was happy to hear from me and invited me in to see him.

After hearing he wanted to build his telemarketing team, I offered to provide marketing consultation and services in telemarketing. I did that off the cuff, but it felt right. He said "Yes!" to me, and my new company came into existence with that first client.

I went home and told my husband, Tony, about the meeting. He knows what life is like with me, and he immediately said okay. The next day when I went into work, I recruited a small team of my best people, and we started working in the evenings to get the new telemarketing operation up and running.

Ok, so here's another example of not necessarily looking for something, but by listening to my intuition and being open to saying "Yes!", a brand-new exciting opportunity was born. This was such a gift because I was able to own my own company, provide extra income to my team that trusted me to be able to grow a new company, and learn how to be an owner/operator. I owe a lot of my success to just paying attention and taking action. The majority of my "wins" were from positions that didn't even exist until I created them, and I need you to understand that we all have this ability. It's not luck or magic, it's your perspective and it's you completely leaning into your superpower.

Don't worry what others are doing and stop comparing yourself. I am not sharing my story so others can copy it, or to make myself feel special. I was compelled to share my story because I now know that we all have the ability to create our ideal life, if we pay attention to the messages that we are given, and we take action by using our unique gifts and superpowers.

Opportunity Is a Click Away

When my employer needed a new system to manage contact relations, I got in touch with a young group of entrepreneurs who were developing a state-of-the-art system.

The problem was their marketing approach. They were sending out CDs to cold contacts to drum up business. It was not working well for them, but I knew I could turn that around. I made my pitch, and they hired my company to consult and help them reach a bigger and more lucrative audience.

I spent a year shuttling between New Jersey and Michigan every other week to work with them on getting their amazing ideas and products out to customers who needed them. It was gruelling for me and Tony, who was holding down the home fort with the kids.

Once again, I learned the value of paying attention and connecting the dots. I was reading the paper one day, and found articles related to a scandal in New Jersey involving sensors used to detect vehicle emissions.

I reached out to my young geniuses in Michigan and, sure enough, they had a product that would work well with the emissions testing. That led to discussions with the security team at the World Trade Center, who were looking for a similar device to look for threats being released into the air in their buildings.

We were also able to offer an artificial intelligence component for a stock trading program, long before anyone talked about AI.

The lesson here is you need to keep your eyes open for opportunities. When you have a goal, you need to be ready to act and believe you are deserving when a chance for something better presents itself. I was able to recognize the new paths opening for me, and see clearly enough to follow them to a successful result.

Beware the Wall

Nelson Mandela once said, "It always seems impossible, until it's done." Sometimes, it may seem there is no other option but to quit. At one time or another, you have run up against a brick wall and thought you needed to give up.

It is critical at this point to stop, breathe, and think about this decision again. Your reptilian brain will step in and tell you to run away to protect yourself. But this might not be necessary, and getting your head clear enough to work it through may reveal a different answer.

Think about it like this: when you are standing in front of a wall, with your nose pressed up against it, you cannot see the door or window that may well be your way to move through and forward. If you step back from the wall and focus on the whole thing, you may be able to see the options in a clearer light and make a better decision based on logic and emotion, instead of letting the self-protective part of your mind guide your choice.

Signs and Signals

It is vital to look for signs that point you forward. Even the tiniest win in a day may be an important clue to unlocking a new opportunity. If you pay attention to small details, a bigger picture is likely to emerge. There will be difficult days, and a lot of thoughts of giving up on those days. Quitting may seem to be the path of least resistance and the easiest option. The thought of leaping into the unknown, while every sense you have is screaming "Danger!" takes courage, as well as the ability to focus on your goal and shut out the noise.

There will be times when quitting is the prudent thing to do, when a situation involves personal safety or the safety and well-being of those you love. Even those decisions require a clear head and careful examination before proceeding, but they are just as valid a choice when made with proper deliberation.

Being Clear and Present

Finding the strength to keep going forward requires clarity and tenacity. You need to clarify your goal. Polish and hone it until it is as clear as a cut diamond. It is important to be focused and precise about what you want and how you want your result to look.

Next, share that goal. Express it to your friends and family. Write it down and look at it everyday to remind yourself of where you are headed. When you understand, and can be clear about where you need to go, your brain will start to help rather than hinder you. The clouds of fear and doubt will lift, and the urge to quit if things become difficult will be more like background noise rather than screaming.

Sharing your goal is critical because, when you share it with others, they may be able to help you achieve it in ways they do not realize.

I always wanted an Arizona office. I had a specific type of space in mind, and shared that goal with a real estate broker I asked to show me some locations. We looked at a few places that were fine, but mundane, and did not match the vision in my head. When we got back to his office, he took a phone call and told me he had learned of a place that might be what I wanted. It was a chance call, but resulted in finding the perfect place to open in Arizona.

By sharing my vision with another person, I was able to get the result I wanted in an unexpected way. Sharing your goal can be advantageous because it opens new paths you might not otherwise have seen or recognized. I threw my goal into the wind and it blew back what I wanted. I believed it would happen, and it did. Do you know why we don't share our dreams with others? It's because we have already concluded that it won't happen, or we are not good enough to receive it. I assure you that if you don't believe strongly enough in your dream to share it, don't bother pursuing it, because it is more than likely not going to happen.

I encourage you, I believe in you, and I know that you can do this…and it all starts with saying "Yes!" to your dreams. Because your perspective and your dream is yours to create, and yours to build, and no one can take that away from you. Say "Yes!" to the life you want, because the only fear you should have is not dreaming big enough.

The Five Second Rule

Mel Robbins wrote a book called *The 5 Second Rule*. Basically, she says when you want to attempt something and a negative voice in your head starts talking, you need to take five seconds before reacting or deciding what to do. Count to five, take a deep breath, and then assess.

The theory is the five second pause is enough to break the negative thought pattern and let you make decisions more clearly and positively. The negative voice is not always a terrible thing. It is there to protect you from things that may genuinely be awful choices. It also activates when the danger is not such that you need to listen so intently.

The little voice may react to something unfamiliar or that will be difficult to do. The important lesson is to learn how to control it, so you can move forward to positive things, even if they are strange or new.

Mistakes Happen

You are going to make mistakes in life, we all have to in order to learn and grow. Accepting this as a fact makes life easier. You are not perfect, and sometimes you must fail to learn how to succeed. I am sharing some of my "highlight" reel with you, but keep in mind that there's always more to the story. Like when I started my own marketing company, and I was traveling back and forth to Michigan every other week. I was bringing in great accounts, but most of the projects were never completed for one reason or another, so I found myself working in the evening again in telemarketing to be able to help Tony with the household expenses, and we were living partially on our savings.

Of course, all these years later it doesn't even seem important. But I want you to know that there really is no such thing as mistakes, they are lessons that we need to experience so we can move into the next phase of our life. Also keep in mind that if you run into a delay, it just means you need to learn something before you move into the cycle of your life. You are a world weaver.

Our natural inclination as humans is to assume everyone else is watching and judging what you do and say. The truth is that everyone has their own struggles, and they are not that invested in what you are doing. You might mess up, feel embarrassed or feel judged. Everyone has felt this way. It is what you tell yourself, and how you press forward, that counts.

Change the Narrative

There are several types of negative self-talk that can be damaging and lead to giving up on your dreams.

Negative thinking is the mindset that declares you are always having problems, and nothing seems to go right, no matter what you do or say.

Remember there are no absolutes in life. Maybe something did not work the first time. The cake fell flat, the test answer was incorrect, or your meeting was dull and attracted criticism.

Getting up, asking for another try, and trying again is almost always an option. Do not let negative thinking stop you from making another attempt. The only time you lose is if you don't get back up and try again.

Next is focusing on negative thinking. This seems obvious, but it needs to be said. If you are so busy looking at all the bad things in the world, you will miss the bright spots. As a result, you will be doing yourself and those around you a disservice.

Good and bad things are always happening. Trying to find a good thing, and turning your energy toward it, is emotionally healthier, and may lead you to something you were previously unable to see. I stopped watching the news years ago, and it has been absolutely liberating. The news media focuses on the negative because that's what provokes an emotional response. I challenge you to turn off negative broadcast news, and seek out good news, because you will be pleasantly surprised how much good there is in the world when the lens through which you are looking filters out the negative.

The worst thing we can do is fall into catastrophic predicting. This occurs when you are constantly worrying that the worst-case scenario is inevitable. Why try, if the outcome will always be the opposite of what you desire?

This kind of thinking can quickly lead to paralysis, and the inability to make good decisions, or recognize positive signs pointing you to a better path. It is better to remember you cannot know the future in any situation. Trying to let things flow naturally would be a more prudent and positive approach to life.

Mind-reading is next on the list. This happens when you assume you know what others are thinking about you, without having any real idea. This kind of assumption may make you hesitate or refuse to ask for what you want, because you think you already know the answer.

Overcoming this presumptive way of thinking can open your mind to new opportunities. Ask another person what they think, or if they have an idea for a course of action, and determine if they can assist you in reaching your goal.

Learning to acknowledge your thinking is important, but training yourself to focus on good and positive things is more vital. Negative thinking and self-talk are limiting and destructive. Everyone falls victim to them from time to time. To break the cycle and keep moving forward, it is critical to pause, adjust, and allow yourself the latitude to assess and decide your next move based on clarity of purpose and courage, as opposed to fear and distrust of your instincts. Say "Yes!" to something, even the smallest "Yes!" will turn your mindset to a more positive channel.

Laura J. Brandao

Chapter 6: It's Time to Ask

"The great secret of getting what you want from life is to know what you want and believe you can have it."
Norman Vincent Peale

The most important thing to remember is: if you do not ask, the answer is already "No."

Asking for things you need or want is not easy. It takes confidence and courage. However, not asking is guaranteeing that you will receive nothing. You can learn how to step forward, trust in the belief that you deserve what you are asking for, and voice that belief to someone in the position to grant it.

One of the first steps to asking is to remember that a "No" is not necessarily a "Never." The timing of your request might be why you are not granted your wish. The person you are asking might not be in the right frame of mind to respond positively. Whatever the reason, it does not mean you should not try asking again.

Pump It Up

The more times you step up and ask for what you believe you deserve, the better your chances are that you will get positive results. Think of asking like working out a muscle. The more you use it, the stronger it gets, and the easier the asking will seem.

The other factor in practicing asking for what you want is that your intuition about how and when to ask will improve. Your confidence will get stronger, and the chance of a "Yes!" will increase along with it.

Timing Is Everything

Along with strengthening your confidence muscle by practicing asking for what you want, you will also hone your intuition on when the timing is best for you to get the "Yes!" you need.

One major factor in asking successfully is gauging the situation in which you are making the request. You should be able to tell the likelihood of getting a positive response by paying attention to the demeanor of the person you are speaking with. Try to ascertain if they seem to be in a good mood, or if they are displaying open and receptive body language.

If someone is smiling and welcoming to you, chances are they are going to be more likely to listen to you with an open mind and heart. If they are scowling and have their arms folded over their chest when you approach them, the time to make your request might not be that particular day.

Find Your "Why" And Expect Nothing

It is important to understand why you are asking for something. Not only does this increase your confidence, but it also transmits sincerity and purpose to the person you are asking.

If you believe in what you are asking for, and know that it will not only benefit you, but those around you as well, that will be apparent and should bring forth a more positive response.

There are four things to keep in mind when asking for what you want.

First, recognize why you are asking. When you take yourself and your ego out of the equation, it is easier to ask because you become fearless when your "why" is transparent. An example would be a mom needing something for her child. She will be less likely to hesitate to ask if her child has a serious need.

Second, ask with confidence. If you believe in what you are requesting, you are more likely to receive a "Yes!" The person being asked will sense if you are authentic and sincere. The feeling they get from you will help them to make their decision. If you are not confident in your request, you can block yourself from getting what you need.

Third, ask without expectation. This is the whole philosophy behind Say YES Everyday. One reason you do not step outside of your comfort zone to ask for what you want is that you let the anticipation of a negative response stop you from trying. Your comfort zone is also a coping mechanism, because you already know what to anticipate.

Keeping score of good versus bad, and expecting positive results based on prior circumstances, can be detrimental to your ability to ask with confidence and certainty in your "why." When you let go of expectation and trust that you are fully within your right to have what you ask for, you will have a far greater impact on the answer you get.

Fourth, have fun with asking. That may sound unrealistic to those who are requesting something of great importance to their life and career. If you go into the situation with a sense of joy and fun, no matter the outcome, you will have made your best effort to gain what you need, and can consider the mere act of asking as a win.

Practice Makes Perfect

The more you practice a skill, the easier it gets. This is common sense, and it applies to asking for things, too. Every time you ask, you get a better idea of what works to get a positive result and what does not.

The experience of asking and having a negative response should be considered a learning experience, and not discounted as a failure. If you can assess what you think made the decision turn against you, change track and try again. You will find your confidence will increase and your results will more likely result in a "Yes!" at the next attempt.

Remember that "No" does not always mean "Never." It could mean "not now" or "not yet." Take the hard "No" out of your self-talk vocabulary, and allow your positivity to infuse your request. You may discover you are more the architect of your own success than the person you are asking.

Follow Up

The follow up is sometimes tougher than the original ask. After you have formally requested something, there may be a stretch of time between asking and getting an answer, whether negative or positive.

Following up is a critical part of the procedure. Most people will make the mistake of assuming that silence means "No." Instead of contacting the other party to check in and inquire, they give up and move on, disappointed by the non-responsiveness.

It pays to remember the other party has their own schedule, life issues, and tasks to complete. Your request is not likely to be at the top of their agenda.

It costs nothing to pick up the phone or open your text or email, and follow up with a polite, cheerful message asking if further information is required, or when to expect a reply to your question. As discussed in a previous chapter, not everyone is focused on you. The person you are waiting on might have forgotten, or might not be able to get to you yet.

By following up politely and positively, you might be in for the pleasant surprise of being granted your request, or being able to cross that item off your task list and move on to bigger and better things. Either way, the matter is settled, and you can stop worrying and start working on your next success.

Define Your Why

When you are a child, you are open and enthusiastic about new things. Whether it is trying a new food or experiencing a new place, your mind is open and learning and enjoying the journey.

As you get older, life's stresses and societal expectations begin to wear down that enthusiasm. They can, if you let them, deprive you of your ability to be open to attempt new things, or step outside your comfort zone and accept failures with grace as learning experiences.

You may also start to assume you will not be granted your requests, and stop asking for what you want and need. You might decide it is easier to settle, and perhaps accept unhappiness or lack of fulfillment as all you deserve.

Even later in life, as you approach and enter middle age, you might wake up one morning, look in the mirror and suddenly wonder why you have let this happen.

The question you should ask yourself is: Why did you wait so long to pursue your dreams, or attempt having what you want and do the things you are passionate about?

It is vital to remember the reason you do things, your "why," is your superpower. It is what sets you apart from others and is the gift you give to those in your life and around you.

Your "why" is the inspiration for your actions, which may inspire others to act on their "why", as well. The energy you put out when following your passion and living your "why" will encourage others to explore their dreams and adventures. It will also make them want to be around you, and feel empowered and free to pursue their "why".

Live Fearlessly

From childhood, I have created and lived my life fearlessly. Everything I have done and every goal I have achieved has been tied to either helping someone else, or being beneficial to more than myself.

Getting out of my comfort zone and asking for what I want with confidence, and bearing the belief that I deserve what I desire, is the key to living in the present and being open to what life has to offer. Others have asked me how I can be so fearless. I would say that fear simply does not exist in my mind. When I hear the word fear, I picture walking on the edge of a mountain or jumping out of a plane, but when it comes to envisioning my best life or acting on an opportunity, that doesn't cause fear.

So, I encourage you to change your mindset because remember, life happens for you not to you, and when you listen and observe, you will clearly see the answers you are searching for to obtain your goals.

Pay It Forward

I want to close this chapter with an example of how defining your "why", and using it to motivate others, is important.

I host a podcast every week called Thrive Thursday. The premise of the show is to spotlight people who have used their creativity and ingenuity to thrive despite the challenges of the current world, and specifically the global COVID-19 pandemic.

I invite a person on the show to talk about how they are surviving and thriving in today's world. That person nominates another person they know to be the guest the following week. I never know who I will be talking with or their background until they call into the show.

I had a young lady as a guest on the show whose name was Koko B. Koko. She started her own fashion line at 27. We had a good interview and she posted on Facebook that she was inspired and motivated by my encouraging words on the show.

I am telling this story not to promote myself, but to emphasize that everyone has the power to lift each other up, and change lives with just a few words.

Koko was starting to feel she was running out of energy and questioning her choices. She was tired and said she had to force herself to take a nap and get ready to talk on the show. Then she wrote how glad she was that she had taken the opportunity and how the energy and content of the conversation had given her new zeal.

In her post, she said, "The moral of this story is the importance of remembering that things are always presented to you for a reason and the best gift you can give to yourself is to show up and be present!"

I was able to give Koko the gift of encouragement. In turn, she gave me a feeling of gratitude that I was able to help her in staying the course toward her goals, and had some small part in moving her forward.

It Is Time

Asking for what you want is hard. It takes practice and the courage to be vulnerable, putting yourself at risk of hearing a dreaded "No."

Once you define your "why", and understand the meaning behind it, the next step is to give yourself permission to receive it. This will allow you to feel confident in asking the next time. Confidence is a muscle that grows stronger with each use.

When you ask for the sake of others and not just yourself, and do so with grace and respect, you may find the world opens up to you in ways you never imagined, and you can pass that success on to others in return.

Continue to ask yourself, "What is about to emerge in my life?" because something new is always emerging. Once you accept that you are in a constant flow of growth and change, there is a positive vibration that will resonate from you that others will be drawn to. Always remember that you are the creator of your life, *not* your circumstances.

Laura J. Brandao

Chapter 7: You Can Never Do It Alone

"If you want to lift yourself up, lift up someone else."
Booker T. Washington

I have an awesome team that has shown me that together we can do anything!

I cannot overemphasize the importance of having a team to help you get through life, whether it is your professional life or your personal life.

Tony

My first and most important team member is my husband Tony. We met as teens and the connection was instantaneous. The first time I saw Tony, I recognized in him a gentle and sweet soul who made me feel comfortable, and he truly understood me. I met him through a friend and it is interesting that it had to be at that specific time. I had just gone through a transformation of losing forty pounds and shedding my girlish awkwardness—emerging as a beautiful butterfly.

One day, my friend asked if I would like to go for a drive with him and his buddy after school. My first reaction was no, but then I learned Tony Brandao was going, and I immediately said "Yes!" We drove around doing errands, and at some point, our friend realized he was the third wheel in the car and decided to go home, leaving Tony and me on our own. Tony turned to me and said, "Hey, do you want to get something to eat?" Without hesitation I said "Yes!"

We had dinner, then drove around town listening to music and talking for hours. With each minute that passed, I was connecting more and more with Tony, knowing deep down I did not want this moment to end. But, at 10 pm it was time to go home. When I got out of the car, something inexplicable and loud inside my head told me to get back in the car and tell him how I felt about him.

I listened to that voice, and it was the first time in my life I said "Yes!" I got back in the car and asked if he wanted to go to the movies that weekend. He agreed and asked for my phone number. From that day on, we have been together. He is my pillar of strength and my most ardent fan. And, it is all because I listened to that inner voice and said "Yes!" to what it was telling me to do.

I think back on that moment and it never ceases to impress upon me the importance of my willingness to take a chance and act on my instinct. My life would be completely different if I had not. I never take for granted the love and support I receive from Tony, or what it has allowed me to accomplish in my life.

Tony and I like to hike together in our free time. While we walk, we talk about everything. We discuss our kids, our jobs, our goals and our dreams. One morning during a hike in Arizona, I asked Tony what he would like to accomplish in the new decade we entered this year. His answer was that he believed he was put on Earth to support me and encourage my endeavours. He is committed to helping me, because he believes in me and my goals, and wants me to succeed.

The feeling I had in that moment was of unconditional love. It was the feeling of someone putting you before themselves in such a genuine and powerful way that you simply cannot see a way to fail at anything. My wish is that you find your Tony, recognize them, and work to make sure you keep them with you on your life journey.

I have been blessed with meeting so many amazing people in my life. In June 2007, during one of the darkest times in the U.S. mortgage market, I was faced with a decision. I could stay at my current mortgage company and hope that everything would work out okay, or I could ask questions and use my network to see if there was an opportunity to land at a safe and secure employer. I decided that I had to bet on myself, so I reached out to a friend in the industry and I said, "Hey, Stacy do you know any 'safe' companies?" She giggled, because believe me no mortgage company was "safe" in mid-2007, but she continued to tell me about a client of hers in Northern New Jersey that was looking to grow a wholesale division. (FYI: A wholesale division is a business-to-business relationship where I, as the lender, works with mortgage brokers to underwrite and close their loans.)

I met with the CEO of American Financial Resources and he told me about his idea of offering one loan program, FHA with credit scores down to a 500FICO score. I would have the opportunity to build a wholesale division from the ground up, every team member, every work flow, etc. But there was no salary, I would be paid entirely by commission.

Okay, let's picture this, I have two kids now in middle school, a mortgage, car loans, etc.; and, the mortgage industry is crumbling and the economy is going towards a recession...but in that moment, all I could think about was the fact that I had the opportunity to build it my way. I jumped in the car and immediately called Tony, and without a moment of hesitation he said, "You are saying Yes!, and I know you will do amazing."

I did say "Yes!", and within a few years we grew the wholesale division to be a top 20 national wholesale lender. In 2009, I was asked to become the first woman partner, and in 2018, I became the first woman president at AFR, and it all started with a "Yes! I couldn't have done it without the phenomenal team that we have assembled, and I would like to recognize a few of them.

Ramona W.

One team member that I'd like to introduce also arrived at AFR due to my willingness to open up and say, "Yes!" I met Ramona when I started AFR Wholesale. She was working for a New Jersey mortgage broker and took a chance on our new wholesale company because she needed a lender who was willing to listen and help a young couple that was trying to get approved for their first mortgage.

Ramona fought hard for her clients. She listened to their needs and advocated fiercely for their success. We worked closely together during that transaction, and I am happy to say we were able to bring the couple home to their first house. A few years passed, and Ramona reached out to see if I had any positions available at AFR. Ramona's passion for helping others resonated with me, and I realized she was an asset I wanted in my organization.

I brought Ramona on board, and shortly after she started a new loan program, the mortgage business exploded. Ramona stepped up and we weathered the storm, and I realized she had been sent to me for a reason. Without her as a team leader, we might not have been able to handle the influx of business. My still, small voice was right again.

Ramona is still with me and we have a connection that gets stronger with time. I trust her to do what needs to be done and she has shown me how use your gut instinct to recruit people. I opened the door to her before I knew how much I needed her, and it was the right call.

Shari M.

My next team member came to me during a difficult time in her life. She had gotten married and she and her husband both lost their jobs at one of the largest mortgage banks in the U.S.

Shari was trained to do conventional loans, but my company runs a different type of loan program. Something about this young woman told me she would be an asset. She was energetic and passionate about people and her career. We decided we could train her to work with our type of loans, and took a chance. She quickly got promoted to team leader.

Shari got pregnant and had her first child. After her son was born, she came into my office and asked to speak with me. She told me she could not leave her son at home. I was dismayed at the thought she would resign but, as a mother, I understood her feelings. I waited with some trepidation to hear what she would say.

She surprised me. She told me she needed the job and income for her family, but she would like me to take a leap of faith and let her work remotely from home. She would come in each evening when her son was sleeping, pick up the files for the next day and drop off the work she completed.

You must understand this was unheard of at that time. Files were all paper, and some were huge. No one was working from home back then, and I wondered how well this would go. However, I knew if anyone could make it succeed, it would be Shari. So, I took a chance and said "Yes!"

I look back now and understand it was Shari's love for her son and my desire to keep a valuable member of my team that drove the decision, and let us explore a new possibility. Shari's willingness to ask for what she wanted, and my willingness to say "Yes!" provided us with a path forward. It was a huge success.

Shari is now vice president of underwriting and a valuable member of my team. If I had not been willing to say "Yes!" I would not have her with me now, helping all of us succeed.

Vickie K.

My Production Coordinator Vickie came to me through an unfortunate circumstance, but she has become one of the most indispensable members of my team.

As my company became busier, I found myself running in all directions, and someone suggested I might need an assistant. I resisted at first, as the idea of asking someone to answer my phone or run errands seemed unpalatable.

However, I soon realized I needed help, so I started interviewing. I had one lovely lady come in and I hired her. Sadly, she was in a serious car accident on the way home from work one evening, and sustained injuries which ultimately took her life. I really liked her, and was shocked and sad. We all were.

I still needed help, and eventually Vickie came to me through another team member who was a friend of hers.

She was out of work, and as soon as I met her, I could sense her nurturing and maternal nature. I felt comfortable with her and hired her.

Vickie calls herself my work mom and she is right. She is always there to listen, give advice, and provide support whether it is business related or personal. She is competent, efficient and loyal. Whatever I need done, she is there and willing to take it on. I have absolute confidence in her ability to get things done and done right.

If it were not for a devastating loss, I might not have been in a position to receive the gift of Vickie in my life. While I wish it had not been a tragedy that brought her to me, I cannot imagine being able to do what I do without her. I learned that letting someone in, and allowing them to help with tasks I might otherwise have tried to do by myself is not only good for me, but also beneficial to them.

Chris L.

I first met Chris when he was a client. He felt a connection to our company and decided to reach out to one of my sales managers to ask if we were hiring. At the time, there were new regulations that were going to make things tough in our industry. I was preparing for a downturn in business and possibly having to lay off some staff.

However, Chris intrigued me, so I agreed to meet with him in my office. I asked him to come in at 7 am one morning. He told me I was the only person who had ever asked him to meet that early in the morning. I am an early bird and it seemed normal to me to meet at that time. He arrived on time and we had a great meeting.

I thought he was great and wanted to hire him, but the timing was so poor, given the circumstances in the mortgage business. I hesitated, but he kept calling and asking to work for me, so I decided that anyone this persistent deserves a chance. I hired him and he was scheduled to start right after Thanksgiving.

One of our company policies is that everyone must take their vacation before the end of the year. When Chris arrived to start work, many of the staff were away for their holidays. Half the team were taking a month off in December, so the office was busy and short staffed.

Chris threw himself in without a backward glance and worked tirelessly to cover for those who were away. I immediately recognized I had hired a superstar; most importantly, whenever I ask Chris if he can get something done, I know it gets done.

Chris is now vice president of operations and a foundational member of my amazing team. He is also a close friend who will always tell me the truth, blunt or not, and keeps me grounded and honest with myself. I could not have grown the company to where we are without him.

Picked For The Team

No matter how I found the members of my team, I cannot imagine my life or success without their love, support and hard work.

Each one came to me at different times and in differing circumstances. However, each time I listened to my instinct telling me I needed them and, in every instance, that instinct was correct.

It takes confidence and courage to recognize we are not meant to do everything on our own. Choosing and retaining a team to provide you with the support and encouragement you need is absolutely necessary to being a success, at whatever goal you are working toward.

I have learned from my team that support is a two-way street. My team wants to be there for me as much as I need them to be. I have come to realize we benefit each other in many ways, and that spreads beyond us, to their colleagues and families as well.

Honesty Is The Best Policy

I believe that, because I chose my team as much as they chose me, we have a synchronized and harmonious relationship that allows for honesty and respect in all our interactions.

When we are working together on a project or task, I have complete confidence that the feedback we give each other will be honest, and accepted as coming from a place of positive and constructive value, not personal power or control. It is not criticism, but feedback necessary to move us forward successfully.

When you have a life and/or work team that is emotionally and intellectually symbiotic, you will find that challenges are less daunting, and the rewards of success are so much sweeter when they are shared.

Being Unapologetically Me

I was on a mentoring call with a young lady who explained that her boss had given her some feedback she did not know how to handle. He told her she was "overwhelming" when she was passionate or speaking animatedly about a subject. He was asking her to tone herself down. She asked me what she should do about this request.

I gave her the same advice I gave myself when someone told me the same thing. Pretending to be someone else is not sustainable. I told her to be herself, whoever that is, and that it is perfectly acceptable to express yourself authentically, despite what others may say or think of you.

Your team should accept you as who and what you are; flaws, foibles and all. You will need to reciprocate in kind, and be open to them in their raw and most authentic form. Only then can you be supportive and supported, and move everyone forward. I know that this is hard to accept and understand, but remember when you show your true self and let your superpower shine, everything else will fall in line for you. Wearing a mask or emulating others will not allow you to become the unique butterfly that the world needs.

Divided You Will Fall

There is no true path to success when you are alone. You may feel you need to do every task on your own to give it value or meaning, but this is not realistic or accurate.

With a supportive and engaged team in your life, you can accomplish so much more than you can alone. The reward is being able to share that success with the people who held you up to get you there.

Whether it is a spouse, partner, friend, parent, child, colleague or someone else, your team can be as small as a party of one, or as large as a company full of people. You will need to lean on them, and they on you, to get where you all want to go.

Be open and receptive when someone comes to you for help, a job or to offer their hand. Having a supportive team around you for all of life's endeavours will make you wonder how you ever managed without them.

No matter how your team comes to you (or you to them), open your mind and heart, and listen to that little voice. It always speaks for a reason.

Chapter 8: Be Memorable – Shine

"There is mighty force, energy, ability inside of us that has not yet been noticed by the world."
Sunday Adelaja

The year 2018 was a transitional one for me. It all began with a phone call from a promoter who asked me to moderate a top originator panel at an event in Irvine, California.

I agreed readily enough but, as I began to think more about it, I realized I had not done this before and I was not sure I could give him the experience he wanted for his audience. I was an executive administrator. I was at my desk at 6 am and worked thirteen or fourteen hours a day. I was not a public speaker.

At the same time, there was a compression in margins in the mortgage business. I was focused on growing the number of loans we were processing to keep my staff busy and my company financially viable. I began to think taking on the panel moderator gig might have been a mistake.

I made an executive decision to send one of my salespeople in my place. He was talented and eloquent, and I had no doubt he would represent me wonderfully and give a masterful performance.

Are You Talking to Me?

A few days later, the promoter called me and asked if it was true that I was sending someone in my stead. I said "Yes!" and that the person I had chosen was perfect for the job. To my surprise, the promoter refused my offer of a qualified replacement outright, and explained he wanted me and no one else. I was slightly taken aback at how adamant he was.

This was a learning experience for me in several ways. As an executive, you get used to those around you saying "Yes!" and doing as you ask. You are not accustomed to having your decisions challenged or refused. The fact that this young man called me out on my decision gave me pause, and encouraged me to step back and think carefully.

I was forced to remove myself from the mindset that all I had to do was ask and someone would do what I wanted without question. It had become easy for me to expect that in my position, so this young guy saying "No" to my decision woke me up. I had to say "Yes!" to this new experience, even though my first instinct had been to delegate. The dynamics of this decision were a refreshing and needed change.

The Next Stage

I decided to throw myself into learning the new skill of public speaking. I uploaded books to my Kindle, watched YouTube videos, and worked at learning techniques, tricks and the art of working an audience. I decided that if I was going to be a moderator, I would be the best one I could possibly be.

I spoke to the promoter and his staff, and asked for the panel members' cell phone numbers so I could speak with them before the event. While I was on the plane flying out to California, I made appointments to meet each of them prior to sharing the stage, so I could get to know them a bit.

I prepared myself in every way I knew how to, so I could do my best job and learn from the experience. I opened myself to an opportunity, and decided to try a new skill that was out of my comfort zone. I found myself enjoying the process.

I was scheduled to follow an energetic motivational speaker who is famous on YouTube. I admit this was a bit daunting, as I would have to up my game and not let the energy in the room drop during my session.

I worked the room a bit during lunch and approached people in the crowd who seemed open and friendly. I introduced myself and chatted a moment or two. If I got a good vibe from them, I asked if they would do me a favor and sit in the front row during my session. I explained that this was my first time in front of an audience and I could use a friendly face to focus on.

The people I asked were surprised, but agreed, and made good on their promise. When I stepped on the stage, I saw a front row of smiling, familiar faces, which gave me a lot of confidence and energy.

Dr. No

My first experience on stage was wonderful! I prepared for it and gave myself the advantage of knowing my panel guests, and positioned an audience row that I could use to help make me comfortable.

The most important takeaway from this story is that none of it would have happened if someone had not said "No" to me at the start. I would have happily passed off this opportunity to someone else, and would never have had the experience or felt the rush of excitement of being in front of an audience and sharing with them.

It took someone saying "No" for me to realize that I should have been sharing this gift with the world long before this moment. We often look for obvious signposts in our business or personal lives. Sometimes it can be the smallest words that carry the most power to spark a change for the better.

Play it Again, Sam

I have had many speaking engagements since that first one. I enjoy sharing with an audience and the adrenaline rush of being on stage and connecting with new people. I make sure to prepare for every possible contingency, and if the unexpected happens, I deal with it accordingly.

I did have one engagement in Las Vegas that might have gone awry, if I had not been able to think on my feet and improvise. This comes with some confidence and practice. When a person who was supposed to be called to the stage was not present, I called up another gentleman with whom I had made eye contact, since he seemed open to some fun.

He worked out perfectly as a spontaneous substitute, and has since become a good client. I was open to a new situation and was able to make the best of what could have been an awkward moment.

Fear Itself

I know that public speaking is one of the number one fears for many people. However, that fear usually stems from what I refer to as the reptilian part of our brain. This part is constantly on alert for danger, and will try to steer us clear of any situation it deems a threat to our well-being.

The key to successfully quieting the reptile brain is preparation. Once you commit to a speaking engagement, your mind will start to cycle through all the things that can go wrong. It will cause stress and worry and will eventually affect your performance, if you let it.

This is why preparation is so important to your success. The most prevalent part of any fear is the unknown. Preparing for an event by removing as much of the unknown as possible will alleviate stress and anxiety, and allow you to fulfill your obligation to the best of your abilities.

It's Not Actually About You

The second important component of being a successful speaker is less obvious, but vital to a good performance.

In short: it is not about you. It is about connecting with your audience and sharing your energy and message with them as a gift. You give the gift of your superpower.

All the overthinking and anxiety caused by the reptilian brain can be tempered by recognizing that sharing your superpower with an audience is offering them something to help them make their lives better.

When you can set your mind in the place that realizes the act of speaking is more about giving to someone else than about yourself, it becomes a joy instead of a chore. The second guessing will disappear, and you will be able to focus on the connection to your audience, instead of your worries. It is an awesome feeling that I would recommend to anyone.

One last thing to remember about the audience is that each person has their own worries, agendas and thoughts. It is, therefore, highly unlikely that everything you do on stage will be subject to the level of intense scrutiny it feels like to you. Relax. You are only one part of each individual's equation!

See And Be Seen

One reason I am sharing this story about my journey to becoming a public speaker is to emphasize the importance for an entrepreneur to be seen and visible in the larger world.

For twenty years, I sat at my desk and grew a successful company. However, I did not know how important it was to be visible until the market was depressed and I needed new growth to keep the company going.

The offer to moderate the panel, and being encouraged to become a public face for my company, was an opportunity I had not considered before, but came to embrace as a benefit to everyone.

As an entrepreneur, you are the face and soul of your company. No one will be able to show your passion and vision better than you. Your current and future clients need to get to know you, not just hear a sales pitch. Open yourself and show your vulnerability, and business relationships will form and grow naturally.

Social media has provided entrepreneurs with the opportunity to share their vision and products to a much wider and diverse audience than ever. It is important, however, to remember that your customers do not only want to purchase your product or service. They also want to learn about who you are as the person who is providing the product or service.

Being open and letting potential customers get to know you takes the courage to be vulnerable. Put a photo of yourself on your website or Facebook page. Write a short paragraph about yourself. You may find that customers are more willing to trust you if they can see you as someone they could know and like.

Let it Shine

One reason that people are drawn to you is the light within you. Letting that light shine and be seen is one of the best ways to build your business and personal network, as well as draw new clients and friends to you.

People have described me as contagious. They tell me they like being around me because I give off a positive energy that makes them feel good. I love making people around me feel better, and in so doing, creating a cycle of positivity and light that benefits me and them.

It may sound ironic these days given the COVID-19 situation, but it is important to figuratively take off your mask and let others see your authentic self, to fully embrace your superpower and share it with the world.

As a child, you are raised to follow a specific pattern of life from school, to work, to having a family and retiring with your partner. But at some point, you might wake up one morning and wonder what you have done with your life.

You are busy and caught up in the chores of living, and you forget who you are and what you're passionate about. You did as you were told; you made a living, raised a family, and now are wondering why you did all those things.

At this point, it is even more important to wake yourself up and spend more time being your authentic self, and share that person with those around you. Remember everything you need to fulfill your "why" is inside of you. You were born with your superpower, and your life up to this point has taught you lessons that prepared you for sharing your gift with the world.

What Next?

During these uncertain times, many people have started recognizing how much more there is to life than just living. You might have discovered new hobbies, passions and pastimes, but you are also learning more about yourself, as the world has become smaller out of necessity.

Careers are important, and so are children and family responsibilities. But losing yourself completely in those parts of life can be too easy, and finding your true self again might be harder than you realize.

Having a purpose in life is one of the most important gifts you can give yourself. By having that purpose, you can find, develop and share your superpower with the world and benefit everyone you offer it to.

Finding your purpose might not happen quickly. It might require patience, and only after years of going through life's more mundane motions can you suddenly discover a path you never noticed before. It might be weedy and overgrown, but it will catch your eye and entice you to follow it deeper and reveal its secrets.

If you keep your mind and heart open to new adventures, you might just find a part of life you never thought you could experience that suddenly becomes accessible and possible. And that part, in turn, could give you and your circle the benefit of enriching your lives and adding to the joy of living. Listen to those little voices, or ideas that come to you when you least expect them, like in the shower or when you are taking a walk. This is where your inspiration will come, and your intention will begin. Become a really good listener to the signs that are around you, and always be willing to take action, because remember that these messages are specifically for you. Don't expect them to be the same as mine or your neighbors.

Chapter 9: Do Not Forget to Listen

"Listen with curiosity. Speak with honesty. Act with integrity."
Roy Bennett

I would like to share a backstory before I discuss my thoughts on listening and how vital it is to your success and relationships in life.

Tonda

In 2019, I was a guest on the Mortgage X podcast. I received several LinkedIn messages afterward, congratulating me and letting me know that listeners had enjoyed the show. One message was from a woman named Tonda who lives in Arizona.

Tonda had worked in the mortgage industry a few years earlier and had noted from the podcast that I had a second home in Arizona. She asked if I would be interested in meeting in person when I was in the state.

I said "Yes!" (of course) and in the spring of 2019, Tonda and I met up and had an amazing discussion. She is a highly motivated, faith-oriented woman who is always looking for ways to change the world.

We talked for hours and found we had a great deal of mutual respect. I asked her what she was looking to do with the rest of her life and then listened carefully to her answer.

Tonda was at a crossroads in her life. She knew she wanted to start her own podcast, and also wanted to get back into the mortgage industry. I asked what was stopping her from moving toward these goals, and she answered me simply and honestly. She told me she had no idea where to start.

I asked her if she would start a podcast with me. She agreed, and we started Positively Charged Biz as a team in July 2019. We wanted to provide the listeners with an experience that left them feeling inspired, and to impart the idea that greatness begins with a pivotal moment when a person decides to act.

Eventually, Tonda found her way back into the mortgage industry. The demands of full-time work and the distances between our workplaces led me to continue the podcast on my own. But the lesson from my experience is that saying "Yes!" will open doors not only for you, but for those you can inspire to say "Yes!" to themselves, as well.

The Importance Of Listening

One thing I discovered from being an executive is that you tend to stop listening. This may be a function of having your staff always looking to you for guidance. It is easy to get into the habit of talking a lot, explaining details and making requests, as well as forgetting how to listen to others when they are trying to communicate their position to you.

When Tonda and I started the podcast, we did so with the agreement we would not interview people from the mortgage industry. There was a good reason for that decision. We both wanted to gain fresh perspectives, and would do so by interviewing guests from vocations outside of our expertise.

By doing this, we gained a larger listening base than just one industry, which provided us with the chance to learn and grow personally, and along with our audience.

To this day when I prepare for my podcast, I read about my guests, listen to their prior interviews, and develop my own questions, so I am prepared to learn more about them than just what they do for a living.

I have learned that when I step outside of my comfort zone, I am forced to listen more carefully, and I become the student instead of the teacher. When you open yourself up to having a student mindset, it can benefit you professionally, as well as in your personal relationships.

If you stop talking and start listening, you will be blown away by what you can learn about another person. This applies even to someone you have known for years and think you know well. You may learn things about your spouse, parent, child, friend or long-term employee that you never noticed or knew. The connections to that person will be positively strengthened by that interaction.

Listening Effectively

Good listening involves more than remaining silent while someone is speaking to you. Good listeners ask questions and provide insight or commentary that promotes a deeper and more insightful conversation.

If you smile and nod your head while someone else speaks, that does not necessarily mean you are absorbing what is being said, nor that you are engaged in the conversation. In a sense, that behavior could be perceived as ignoring the speaker, as you are not contributing in any way, but are merely present as sound is being shared in your direction.

I have also learned that asking questions and staying curious actually reduces stress. My favorite story about listening and staying curious is Ray Kroc's. He was a 50-year-old milk shake salesman that received an order for 8 machines at one restaurant. Now, he could have just placed the order and moved on but NO, he asked questions and he scheduled an appointment to fly out to meet the restaurant owners, the McDonald brothers, so he could better understand their operation. Wow, imagine that the entire fast-food industry would have been different if Ray Kroc didn't listen, ask questions and take action.

We all have these moments, but most of the time we just place the order and move on. But I know that if you are reading this book, you want more, you expect more, and you are destined for more.

Not a Defensive Posture

An ineffective listener would be someone who aggressively asks questions, or tries to persuade the speaker that their position is invalid or incorrect. If the listener takes a defensive or aggressive stance, it is a clear indicator they are not engaging in a conversation as much as they are competing with the speaker.

Making suggestions for the speaker to consider is a more effective way of engaging in the conversation, and letting them know you are open to their story without judgment.

Good listeners do not listen while actively trying to form a response before the other party has finished speaking. They listen from a student point of view, to learn from the speaker before forming and relaying a thoughtful response.

Learn How to Listen

Effective listening is a skill that requires practice. It is important to have a genuine interest in what the other person has to say. If you are bored to death of the topic, it might be difficult to maintain your focus. Practicing having the mindset of a student will be helpful in being able to concentrate, even if you are less than excited by the subject matter.

My modus operandi for listening when I am not sure I have interest in the subject, is to focus on my interest in the person speaking. I want to feel better about having learned something new after the conversation, so I make that my mindset going in. If I listen well, I should have no problem learning a new detail about the person, or something I did not know before.

That technique ensures my attention will be properly focused and engaged in the conversation, and that both parties will benefit. The party I am speaking with and listening to will have their story heard respectfully, and I will have discovered something new about either the speaker or their topic.

It is Still Not About You

I have made this point before about public speaking. The discussion is not about you or what you are saying, doing or thinking in that moment.

When you are actively engaged in listening to another person, you need to remember that this process is not about you. If you have an earnest question for the other party, based on what you are hearing and thinking about, then ask it.

Ask your question without worrying about being judged, or perceived as uninformed or obtuse. If you are listening to someone while simultaneously wondering how to ask your question without looking silly, you cannot listen to them effectively.

Being fully present and engaged in listening means thinking about their story, not yours. Adopting this mindset as an active listener takes practice and time to develop as a skill, but it is worth the effort. You will learn a new and valuable skill for yourself, and will provide the speaker with a rewarding and confidence-building experience.

115

People Are Important

This is important to me and I want to share my thoughts on this subject in the context of relationships with other people.

Humans have a short period of time in this world. I love people and it saddens me to see so many people struggle, or spend valuable time caught in the hamster wheel of the mundanities of life, instead of living every moment to its fullest.

In the opening chapters of this book, I said that we are all unique and we are winners from the moment we are born. The number of unique circumstances that create each of us is mind-boggling. I cannot imagine anyone has been born without a specific purpose or gift to share with the world.

I want you to recognize your uniqueness and understand the gifts inside you. I want you to discover the joy of sharing those gifts with others to enrich their lives, as well. Once you find and turn on that switch to your inner light, it will draw others to you and make your life more fulfilling.

Good Listening is a Superpower

Being a good listener is a superpower you can develop and practice when you subscribe to the notion that all people are worthy of being heard and understood.

Giving another person the gift of your time and your full attention can have surprising results for both of you. You show respect for another person by being fully present and focused on what they have to say. Asking good, meaningful questions to fully understand their point of view offers them the wonderful feeling of being heard.

As a good and effective listener, you will receive not only the gift of learning something you did not know before, but you will also receive the speaker's trust. It can take courage to share a personal point of view, especially if the subject is personal or controversial.

Having an earnest and deep conversation with another person is a balancing act of hearing, thinking and responding. The art of human communication requires a speaker and a listener. Learning how to perform both sides of that equation with skill and grace takes effort and practice, but is also immensely rewarding.

Life is about communicating, and effective listening should be a goal you aspire to in your personal and professional lives.

My charge to you is to find someone you care about and ask them to talk to you about something they are passionate about. Listen carefully, ask good, meaningful questions, and feel your connection to that person grow, along with your understanding of something new.

Chapter 10: Thrive Thursdays

"Sometimes you need a little crisis to get your adrenaline flowing and help you realize your potential."
Jeannette Walls, The Glass Castle

While I am not suggesting the COVID-19 pandemic is a "little crisis," I would posit to you that a crisis, large or small, can provide a push to get you moving in a different or more positive direction.

The Beginning

When the pandemic hit in early 2020, no one knew what was going to happen. Everyone felt fear and apprehension, and it was difficult for many people to plan how they were going to survive.

Jobs disappeared; panic buying ensued; and bills began to mount. It was incredibly stressful and terrifying for most of us. We woke up each morning worried and went to sleep at night the same way. It was exhausting and disheartening to have the world turned upside down in what seemed like the blink of an eye.

During the first weekend of the shelter-in-place notices, I got a phone call from a colleague. She was panicking and I was her usual go-to person for a positive message and some optimism. This time was different, because I was also uncertain of what was going to come.

We were both anxious and upset, and suddenly she had an idea. She suggested we go on Facebook Live to share how we were feeling. Since no one knew how to handle this crisis, maybe letting others know they were not alone in how they were feeling would help them, and us too.

The next Thursday, we went live and decided that the people we spoke to each week would nominate the interviewees for the next week. Every week from March until September, we had three new people on each session. We called it" Survive and Thrive."

Change Up

After that first 25 weeks, I realized that my guests were not just surviving—they were thriving! They had each risen to the challenge of this new world with creativity and energy, and were moving forward in many different ways.

The guests we interviewed up until September were all in the mortgage business. That is my industry, so it seemed that each guest nominated someone else in the same field. It was not intentional, but evolved that way.

On September 10, 2020, I changed the name of the segment from 'Survive and Thrive' to 'Thrive Thursdays' www.thrivethursday.org, and began interviewing people outside the mortgage industry. That changed the dynamic of the segment and opened up a new world to me and my guests.

Two Questions

The other major change I made to the show format was to ask each guest two specific questions. First, I would ask them what they had said "Yes!" to that led them to start thriving. Second, I would ask what they thought was their superpower, or special gift that they could share with the world.

The first question seemed easy to answer. The responses included starting a new exercise routine, spending more time with family and other positive life changes.

The second question, however, seemed to be significantly difficult for most guests. It is understandable, as most people do not like to sound like they are tooting their own horn, so to speak. But I quickly realized that it can be detrimental to a fulfilling life to not be aware of your gifts and be able to use them.

I started prepping guests with a pre-call, and made sure to ask them to think about that second question prior to being on the show. I told them to ask a loved one in their life to tell them what they think their superpower is.

A person who loves you will be able to see things in you that you either do not recognize, or have not thought about before. The strategy worked extremely well. My guests were usually astonished at the information they gleaned by asking the question of a spouse, partner, or other significant person in their life.

One woman cried because her grown sons were so effusive in expressing their love and admiration when they told her how they felt about her. She was overwhelmed by their response, and grateful for the opportunity to learn how her sons see and feel about her.

Building A Community

As the show has progressed, I have found that asking guests to discover, recognize and accept their unique gifts has had an impact far beyond what I imagined.

I saw light begin to shine within people who were sharing their discovery, and it was awe inspiring and beautiful to see. It often felt like they were seeing themselves for the first time, and looking at themselves through the eyes of those they love.

Something else was happening, too. I began to see a community forming. The guests we had on the show were tuning in to listen to each other's segments. Some contacted each other to offer support, or ask for support from those they felt a kinship with.

People who would never have crossed paths in life were now connected, and forming new connections that created benefit and opportunity they might not have had or considered otherwise.

The connections and networks that were forming crossed all lines of ethnicity, gender, age and vocation. There was an up swell of communication between people across the country who were drawn to each other's light, and reached out to share with others and benefit from them, as well. The community has become so strong that I have decided that the second Say YES Everyday! book is going to be "Say YES Everyday! Everyone has a story."

How could I go through the process of writing this book, encouraging you to listen and take action, and not realize that I need to share my Thrive Thursday guests with the world in a bigger way? I am once again saying "Yes!" to using my voice and my superpower to make a positive change in the world. Remember we all have different gifts, so although a Live show and a book are my vehicles to reach others, that doesn't mean they have to be yours. Be open to varied methods and know that there is no wrong way, you just need to find your way.

Stringing The Lights

As the show has continued, so has the string of beautiful lights that sparkle each time a new guest comes on to share their experience of finding their superpower. The sharing encourages others to step forward, and the next light comes on.

So many people from different walks of life have talked about how they found their light, and finding it made it more important to share it and watch it grow.

Each light that shines anew lights the path for the next, and I know the continuity of that path will continue.

The Power Of Positivity

I want to emphasize the importance of maintaining positivity, especially now with the world upside down for so many people. Sharing, connecting and giving the gift of your superpower to the world may seem like a small thing, but it might be what makes someone else's life change for the better.

While doing the Thrive Thursdays show, I have found that everyone is the same in some fundamental ways. You each have the ability to change the world in some way. By sharing your talent, you contribute to a better experience for yourself and for others.

The most common superpower I hear about from my guests is that they are positive and optimistic people who make those around them feel better and more hopeful about life. Being able to affect someone that way is powerful. Knowing you are the person who can do that is a wonderful discovery to make about yourself.

My Dream

I began the Thrive Thursday journey as a response to the pandemic crisis and how it was affecting me and those in my tribe.

As it progressed through months of anxiety and uncertainty for people in their personal and professional lives, and changed how they lived day to day, I began to sense there was more to this movement than survival.

You survive each day by having your basic necessities of life met. However, to thrive beyond mere survival takes creativity and a willingness to say "Yes!" to things you might have otherwise avoided, from either fear or lack of confidence.

When I saw how my guests were not only surviving the pandemic world, but actively finding ways to thrive despite the restrictions and fear, I knew I had to find out how they were doing it, and share those stories as far and wide as possible.

What emerged was a fundamental shift in the show's tone and nature from surviving to thriving, and all the optimism and energy that comes with the ability to make the best of a bad situation with grit and fortitude.

I have met people whom I might never have had the chance to meet in my path of life, and have learned from them in many amazing ways. Along the way, I have heard stories of love, strength and ingenuity.

Every story has a common thread. It is to say "Yes!" to a new way of discovering individual gifts that will provide the world with a collective aura of light that draws others to it, and gives them the chance to feel a part of the larger human community and contribute in their own way.

My dream for everyone is encompassed in the premise of Thrive Thursdays: to find your gifts, learn to use them often and share them with others to enrich everyone's lives.

I have met many amazing and diverse people due to Thrive Thursdays. Each person is unique and has displayed the ability to work toward their goals despite the current conditions.

When the world does tilt back onto its proper axis, these wonderful people will continue to inspire, connect and thrive. I want to continue interviewing individuals nominated by their predecessors to keep the network expanding and encompassing as many people as we can.

Take a moment and ask someone who loves you to tell you what your superpower is. Say "Yes!" to finding out what makes you special in the eyes of another person, and I promise you the reward will be worth the effort.

Laura J. Brandao

Chapter 11: Say YES Everyday!

"Say yes and you'll figure it out afterwards."
Tina Fey

We have come to the final chapter of the book. Before we wrap up, I want to review and make sure the message has been received.

To live the life you want and deserve, you need to learn to use the word "Yes!" everyday. That word should become your talisman, your touchstone and your mantra, from the moment you open your eyes to the sunshine to the minute you close them to the stars at night.

I wrote this book because I needed to share this idea with you. I want you to live your best life and feel happy and fulfilled. I am a people person by nature, and have discovered that the secret to my happiness each day is helping others find theirs.

Learn Your Lesson

I have talked about many ways to say "Yes!" and get what you want out of life.

Learning from failures is an important way to avoid getting stuck in place when you are yearning to move forward. It is critical to change your mindset, so you can see a failure as a lesson in how to succeed in your next attempt, instead of a finite ending to your endeavor. I will give an example of how to look at a failure.

Imagine you are a successful businessperson with a large organization you built from scratch. You have great employees, and your company is expanding and thriving. You have a great network of friends and colleagues with whom you work and socialize. You think of some work colleagues as friends.

On one occasion you make a mistake. It is a social mistake and not intended to cause harm or upset anyone. It might be a slip of the tongue or a misguided email that ends up on the wrong screen. It happens to all of us at some point in our lives, and how we handle it tells us what we need to learn.

How do you handle this? You have hurt or upset someone you care about, and it is also related to your business. You could throw up your hands and hide from the public. You could get angry at the other party for being too sensitive and end the relationship. Or, you could face the situation, acknowledge it was a mistake, and effectively communicate your error and the fact that you have learned from it and it will never happen again.

All these options are open to you, but you need to choose one. Find the lesson in the error and use that lesson to mitigate the current situation, and avoid it ever happening again. The option you choose will dictate your path forward.

The important message is to be open to saying "Yes!" to correcting the error as best you can and, whatever the outcome, using the lesson learned to move past it. The original mistake was a failure to communicate effectively, but that should not mean everything comes to a crashing halt, unless you let it.

Learn from failure. Accept it as part of life; absorb the lesson it teaches no matter how painful or difficult, and use the lesson to avoid making the same mistake again. Turn the negative into a positive, and life will become easier as you move forward.

Sometimes in life, you need to lose some things to grow and focus on new and better. That can include people you thought were important to you, but ultimately proved to only be with you for part of your life's journey. As hard as that can be to accept, it pays to learn how to find the positive in the most painful lessons. I have also seen that when we do trip up, you will see who your true supporters are, and those that were with you as long as they were positively benefiting from the relationship. As we go through our seasons of life, people will come and go, and it's ok to outgrow some relationships. This is all part of growing and learning.

Subscribe To A Tribe

Failure is hard to accept. Lessons may be hard or painful to learn. But life without a tribe to rely on, confide in and manage to succeed with, is virtually impossible.

I spoke about my team earlier in the book. My team includes my husband, my work family, and my loved ones. They are all a huge part of who I am and how I have found success in business and in life.

You need to have a tribe of people around you who will guide, encourage, love and support you in all the things you do. Without a tribe, you will not be able to see yourself as others do, making it more difficult to learn how special and unique you are. Your tribe is the mirror in which you need to recognize yourself, especially when life is challenging.

Your tribe can also be your conscience when you face ethical or moral dilemmas and are not sure which way to turn. They know you well and they know your heart. Trusting your tribe to remind you of who you are and what you stand for will help you to choose the right path for you, and for whomever your actions may impact.

It is easy to get lost in trying to do everything by yourself. Women can be particularly prone to this habit. You might not think you need to ask for help, even though you need assistance. Eventually, you will burn yourself out trying to handle everything alone and not inconvenience anyone else.

The lesson to learn from neglecting to lean on your tribe when needed is that you end up being of no use to anyone, even yourself, if you become so exhausted and overwhelmed that you cease to function effectively at any task.

Your tribe wants to help and support you. They care about you and may feel honored to be asked for help. When you assume that your request will be regarded as inconvenient, stop and remember that if someone asks you for help, you would gladly pitch in, even if it takes you away from your own task.

It is important to show your tribe the same respect, and honor them with allowing them to help someone they care about. Sharing a burden or chore will lighten your load and give someone else the chance to show you they care enough to help. It is a mutually beneficial situation, and should be considered that way, instead of an imposition.

I went through this exercise in my life. When I started my business, I wanted to do everything myself. I felt uncomfortable asking someone else to do the routine things that needed to be done, because I thought it might be insulting to them.

As things got busier, I found I was less effective at getting things done, because I would start a task and the phone would ring and distract me, causing me to lose track and have to start again. It slowed me down and affected my ability to work. I was told I needed an assistant, but I refused because I felt that I should do these tasks myself.

Eventually, I began to realize I did need help. I needed someone to take on some of the distracting things, so I could focus on the larger issues and move the company forward. I hired an assistant to answer the phone, take messages and handle the smaller day-to-day tasks I could not keep up with.

Saying "Yes!" to getting help proved to be the right thing to do. I added a valuable and much-loved member to my tribe. I also lightened the weight of the tasks that I needed to do, which allowed me to focus on the things I do best, and move us in the right direction.

Having a team or tribe to help you reach your goals is a gift that you and your tribe give each other everyday. Letting someone in and asking for help when you need it is wise, and generous to those who love you and want to be a part of who you are and what you do everyday.

When you gather your tribe around you and share the joys, pains and successes of life, you enrich your experience as well as theirs, and strengthen the bonds between you in ways you cannot imagine until you try.

Don That Cape

The most important message I want to impart to you is to find, recognize and use your superpower.

You are born a winner. You win by being born. The number of seemingly random events that must occur for you to even exist is staggering. When you understand that, you will realize how unique and special every person in the world is.

I have said that every person has a superpower. You have at least one gift that you are given innately, and you should share it with the rest of the world. To my core, I believe that you must discover your gift, use and hone it, and then project it into the world to make everyone better.

The first thing you must do is give yourself permission to realize how special you are and accept that fact with your whole heart. Recognizing the absolutely unique and beautiful being you are will open you up to looking for ways to use your gifts in new and rewarding ways. Your superpower will grow and get stronger if you share it over and over again with those you encounter, whether they are a stranger or someone you know and love.

When you say "Yes!" to your superpower and the awesome power you can wield, you will feel a shift in your life from just doing to being who you are. Getting lost in the mundane chores of life and believing they are the only thing to focus on is a mistake most people make until far too late in life.

Work is no more than the vehicle to your evolution as a human being. You need to make money to pay the mortgage, feed, clothe, and educate your children and provide some comforts for your family.

The real trick is to also make looking after yourself a priority. When you spend time taking care of yourself physically and mentally, you will be in the best condition and strong enough to provide the care and attention others need from you too.

There are times when you may find yourself in a dark place. You will wake up in the morning and cannot seem to find the light to guide you to get out of bed, stretch and smile when thinking about the day ahead. This can happen gradually without you knowing it until one day, it overwhelms you and you shut down. You will be confused as to how you arrived at this point.

The key to coming through the dark and reaching the light again is to recognize and accept yourself for the miracle you are, and use that to positively affect those around you. Giving to others is the best gift you can give yourself, and it becomes almost addictive, once you start to see what you are capable of.

The Hope Dealer

I want to share the story of Marissa, one of my Thrive Thursday guests, to illustrate the awesome potential when you find, recognize and begin to use your superpower.

Marissa is a young wife, mother and nurse. She is happily married and enjoys her work and her family.

Marissa is also a cancer survivor. She was diagnosed as a young mother and fought for her life with everything she had. Even on her darkest days, she kept on fighting. Somewhere in the midst of the fear, pain and fatigue, Marissa found hope. And with it, she found her superpower.

Marissa is a nurse by profession, so she cares for other people everyday. On her cancer journey, she discovered that sharing her experience could inspire others and give them hope. She started speaking to groups about surviving cancer and the light at the end of the tunnel.

The more Marissa shared her superpower with others and helped them to find their hope, the better her life became. Since winning her battle with cancer, Marissa has gone on to have another baby. She also found a passion for making and selling costume jewelry.

She told me she had always classified herself with labels. She was the preacher's daughter, a wife, a mother and a nurse. But she never felt like Marissa. After her journey with cancer and the awakening of her superpower, she started to recognize her true self. She is now authentically Marissa, with all the wonderful things that she is and has accomplished.

Marissa calls herself a "hope dealer." She shares her ability to maintain strength and faith in the face of some of life's worst moments. With that sharing, she inspires, comforts, and offers hope to those who need it the most. It is a gift that benefits her and her listeners in so many positive ways.

Marissa is a perfect example of how recognizing and using your unique superpower can transform your life in ways you cannot imagine. Using that superpower more often intensifies the effects, and you may wonder why you waited so long to find and use it. I also realize that it was important for me to meet Marissa as I was writing this book, so I could share her story with the world. That is another example of the gifts we can receive when we are paying attention, and open to receiving them.

What I Most Want For You

So here we are at the end of this book. These are the final words of our journey. I have shared something I fully believe in and that is close to my heart.

I discovered my superpower is spreading positivity and giving others the confidence to find their own superpower. I am happiest when I energetically pursue my vision with the people I love by my side, and everyone that comes into my world feels energized and empowered. When I speak or meet with someone, whether it's the first time or I have known them forever, I want them to walk away from our connection feeling positive, inspired and confident. I challenge myself to make that happen everyday.

I want you to feel that elation and fulfillment, and I want you to stop postponing your joy. As soon as you finish reading this book, I want you to go to someone who loves you and ask them what they think your superpower is. Listen carefully to what they say and put that information into practice as often as you can. Keep in mind that we have multiple powers, but start with one and grow it from that point.

There is no right or wrong answer. Your superpower is uniquely yours. Give yourself permission to share it as far and wide as you can, and experience the joy and energy that comes with that sharing.

Using your superpower will help you to live the best version of you that you can be. It will benefit you and those you love in your life. They will see the new light in your eyes and want to know your secret. You can share your secret with them, and watch their transformation as they unleash the power within them.

If you have read this book to the end, you did it because you were ready for something new. You were curious enough to pick it up and look for something better to say "Yes!" to in your life. I encourage you to say "Yes!" to love, to abundance, to compassion, to gratitude, and say "Yes!" to service to others. Keep creating and asking yourself, "How can I grow, give and celebrate every single day on Earth by saying Yes?"

You are not here to get something out of life, you were born to let your superpower out. Set it free because the world needs your gift, and everything you hope and desire is already here for you, you just need to be ready to receive it.

Everything you have done up to this point in your life has prepared you for this moment. There is a reason why you decided to read this book. Nothing happens by accident. I would love to hear your "Yes!" stories, and you are now officially part of the Say YES Everyday! community and tribe. I am so proud of you and I know there is greatness within you.

www.sayyeseveryday.com

Email: laura@sayyeseveryday.com

Facebook: Sayyeseveryday

Laura J. Brandao